MUSEUM MONOGRAPHS

WINERY, DEFENSES, AND SOUNDINGS AT GIBEON

By

JAMES B. PRITCHARD

With Contributions by William L. Reed,
Douglas M. Spence, and Jane Sammis

PUBLISHED BY

THE UNIVERSITY MUSEUM

UNIVERSITY OF PENNSYLVANIA

1964

Price $3.50

Please send orders for *Museum Monographs* to

The University Museum,
33rd and Spruce Streets,
Philadelphia, Pennsylvania 19104

CONTENTS

INTRODUCTION

Although the southern hill at el-Jib had been occupied intermittently from the Early Bronze Age down through Byzantine times, the debris of occupation — where the best evidence for a city's history is usually to be found — is scant and poorly stratified. Wind, rain, and the depredation by stone-looters have combined to denude the mound of much of the evidence for its past. In general the chief periods of occupation have become clear during the five seasons of excavations, but it has been impossible to find traces of each of these periods in every area. Obviously parts of the mound settled in some periods were deserted in others. In view of this somewhat erratic pattern of the stratigraphic evidence for the history of the mound, it has been deemed impracticable to assign letters or numbers to the general strata and to present the evidence in the final reports under a chronological arrangement. Rather, we have considered it feasible to present the results arranged according to topics of importance, such as the inscribed jar handles (*Hebrew Inscriptions and Stamps from Gibeon*, 1959), the stepped tunnel and the pool-and-stairway (*The Water System of Gibeon*, 1961), and the rock-cut tombs to the west of the hill (*The Bronze Age Cemetery at Gibeon*, 1963). In the present work the aim has been to document the discoveries of the winery and the systems of defense — topics likely to be of interest to students of the archaeological history of Palestine — and to present in detail the results of three soundings which supplied the best evidence for the history of occupation at the site.

Almost as important as the choice of the areas of a large mound to be excavated is the decision as to what — and how much — of the evidence found should be published. Besides the material presented here and in the preceding monographs there remain unpublished some plans of walls, catalogues of pottery, and some field notes upon a few areas where excavation was carried out, but in which there appeared material of very limited interest or artifacts which merely duplicated those which came from plots which have been chosen for publication. In the appendix we have given a list of plans and sections which are stored in the files of the University Museum of the University of Pennsylvania, Philadelphia, where they may be consulted by interested scholars.

One other decision we have made should be a matter of record. The advantages of publishing the results of an excavation promptly are obvious. Notes are more useful when they are fresh and when the supervisors who wrote them can be called upon — as they have been on a number of occasions during the preparation of this monograph — for help in reconstructing details which were overlooked in the harrowing days of field activity. Equally obvious, however, is the price which must be paid for a relatively prompt publication: the inability to draw all possible conclusions, to cite every parallel and analogy, and to push the research upon the many details to the limits of possibility. Faced by this choice we have decided to publish promptly — not hastily we trust — our plans, drawings, photographs, sections, notes, and catalogues. We have listed some of the basic parallels and written a minimum of notes and have left to the interested student the task of giving more complete answers to some of the questions raised by the discoveries.

The results from the first four of the five seasons at el-Jib were presented in popular form in the writer's *Gibeon, Where the Sun Stood Still*, Princeton, 1962, which was written before the final season in the summer of 1962. In that season the excavation centered primarily in the tomb area to the west of the tell and at the northwest section of the tell itself, where the most complete evidence for the two major defensive systems was found. Thus in this monograph we are able to carry the subject of defenses along further than we did in the book.

It is a happy duty to acknowledge the generous cooperation of the Department of Antiquities of the Kingdom of Jordan throughout the entire period of our excavations at el-Jib. They were begun when G. Lankester Harding was the director, proceeded under the directorship of Said Durra, and were finished while Dr. Awni Dajani was in charge of the Department of Antiquities. It has been a pleasure to work with each of these three men, and especially Dr. Dajani, who smoothed the way for the work during the last three campaigns. In addition to the inspectors of the Department of Antiquities assigned to the staff, and mentioned in the list of staff members, mention should be made of the helpful service of Sami Meddah, who proved invaluable in many crises during the long, hot summers at el-Jib. The Department of Antiquities and its staff proved to be not only our genial hosts during the five seasons in Jordan, but competent colleagues in the work of excavation.

In addition to the field staff listed on p. 65, mention should be made of a research staff collected at the Church Divinity School of the Pacific, Berkeley, California, during June, July, and August of 1961. During that summer much of the preliminary work on the text and plates of this monograph was done. William L. Reed, Douglas M. Spence, Jane Sammis, George W. Tuma, David Green, Hope Athern, and Mary Pritchard made various contributions such as preparing preliminary drafts from field notes, drafting, cataloguing, and preparing plates for the publication. More recent contributions to this report have been made by Joanna A. Fink, who served as a student assistant during 1963-64, Barbara S. Baker, who typed and prepared plans and drawings, and Geraldine Bruckner, who has been a constant source of help in matters of editing and publishing.

To no small degree has the success of the el-Jib project been due to the encouragement and help of Froelich Rainey, director of the University Museum, throughout the entire span of years, extending from 1955, when the first plans were laid, until their completion in 1962. The American School of Oriental Research in Jerusalem was a cooperating partner in the project and provided useful equipment for the excavation and housing for the staff; in 1956 and 1957 the University Museum was joined by the Church Divinity School of the Pacific, Berkeley, California, as one of the sponsors.

The threads of the authorship of this monograph are difficult to disentangle. William L. Reed prepared the preliminary draft of the sections entitled "The Rock-cut Cellars," "Contents of the Cellars," and "Iron Age Houses in Area 17" during the summer of 1961; Douglas M. Spence described from supervisor's notes the soundings in Trench I and Area 15-K/L-18 during the same summer; and Jane Sammis prepared the "Catalogue of Coins." After the 1962 campaign, when a wealth of new material became available, the writer revised considerably each of these sections, with the exception of the "Catalogue of Coins," making use of newer information and normalizing the scheme of presentation to fit it into the remaining material for which he was solely responsible. Since this is a work of composite authorship, the writer must assume responsibility for the entire work, with its errors and mistakes, and acknowledge with gratitude the vast amount of labor done by those who first put the material into manuscript form.

The objects listed in the catalogues opposite the plates of drawings and photographs are now in the University Museum of the University of Pennsylvania, Philadelphia, with the exception of those claimed by the Jordan Government for the National Museum in Amman. These are marked "Amman" in the catalogue. A few heavy objects which could not be transferred easily to Philadelphia are stored temporarily in the storage room of the American School of Oriental Research, Jerusalem.

ABBREVIATIONS

AASOR	*Annual of the American Schools of Oriental Research*
ANS	American Numismatic Society
APEF	*Annual of the Palestine Exploration Fund*
AS IV	Elihu Grant and G. E. Wright, *Ain Shems Excavations*, Part IV (Pottery), Haverford, 1938
AS V	Elihu Grant and G. E. Wright, *Ain Shems Excavations*, Part V (Text), Haverford, 1939
BA	*The Biblical Archaeologist*
BASOR	*Bulletin of the American Schools of Oriental Research*
Beth-zur	O. R. Sellers, *The Citadel of Beth-zur*, Philadelphia, 1933
BIES	*Bulletin of the Israel Exploration Society*
BMGC Pal.	G. F. Hill, *Catalogue of the Greek Coins of Palestine*, London, 1914
Bronze Age Cemetery	James B. Pritchard, *The Bronze Age Cemetery at Gibeon*, Philadelphia 1963
Cohen	H. Cohen, *Description historique des monnaies trappées sous l'Émpire Romain*, VII (2nd ed.) Paris and London, 1888
Discoveries in the Judaean Desert II	P. Benoit, O.P., J.T. Milik, and R. de Vaux, O.P., *Les Grottes de Murabba ͨat*, Oxford, 1961
Gezer II	R.A.S. Macalister, *The Excavation of Gezer*, Vol. 2, London, 1912
Gezer III	R.A.S. Macalister, *The Excavation of Gezer*, Vol. 3, London, 1912
Gibeon	James B. Pritchard, *Gibeon, Where the Sun Stood Still: The Discovery of the Biblical City*, Princeton, 1962
Hazor I	Yigael Yadin, et. al., *Hazor I*, Jerusalem, 1958
Hazor II	Yigael Yadin, et. al., *Hazor II*, Jerusalem, 1960
Hebrew Inscriptions	James B. Pritchard, *Hebrew Inscriptions and Stamps from Gibeon*, Philadelphia, 1959
IEJ	*Israel Exploration Journal*
Jericho I	Kathleen M. Kenyon, *Excavations at Jericho*, Vol. 1, Jerusalem, 1960
Kindler	A. Kindler, "The Jaffa Hoard of Alexander Jannaeus," *IEJ*, Vol. 4, 1954, pp. 170-185
Lachish II	Olga Tufnell, et. al., *Lachish II: The Fosse Temple*, London, 1940
Lachish III	Olga Tufnell, *Lachish III: The Iron Age*, London, 1953

Lachish IV	Olga Tufnell, et. al., *Lachish IV: The Bronze Age*, London, 1958
Meggido I	R. S. Lamon and G. M. Shipton, *Megiddo I: Seasons of 1925-34, Strata I-V*, Chicago, 1939
Megiddo II	Gordon Loud, *Megiddo II: Seasons of 1935-39*, Chicago, 1948
Megiddo Tombs	P. L. O. Guy, *Megiddo Tombs*, Chicago, 1938
NZ	*Numismatische Zeitschrift*
Qasile	B. Maisler, *The Excavations at Tell Qasile*, Jerusalem, 1951 (Reprinted from *IEJ*, Vol. 1, 1950-51)
QDAJ	*Quarterly of the Department of Antiquities of Jordan*
QDAP	*Quarterly of the Department of Antiquities in Palestine*
RB	*Revue Biblique*
Reifenberg	A. Reifenberg, *Ancient Jewish Coins*, Jerusalem, 1947
RIC	*The Roman Imperial Coinage*
Samaria III	J. W. Crowfoot, G. M. Crowfoot and Kathleen M. Kenyon, *The Objects from Samaria, Samaria-Sebaste, No. 3*, London, 1957
Svoronos	Ioannos N. Svoronos, *Ta nomismata tou kratous ton Ptolemaion*, Athens, 1904
TBM I	W. F. Albright, *The Excavation of Tell Beit Mirsim in Palestine, Vol. 1: The Pottery of the First Three Campaigns*, AASOR, Vol. 12, New Haven, 1932
TBM Ia	W. F. Albright, "The Excavation of Tell Beit Mirsim, Ia: The Bronze Age Pottery of the Fourth Campaign," in AASOR, Vol. 13, pp. 55 ff., New Haven, 1933
TBM II	W. F. Albright, *The Excavation of Tell Beit Mirsim, Vol. II: The Bronze Age*, AASOR, Vol. 17, New Haven, 1938
TBM III	W. F. Albright, *The Excavation of Tell Beit Mirsim, Vol. III: The Iron Age*, AASOR, Vol. 21-22, New Haven, 1943
TN I	C. C. McCown, *Tell en-Nasbeh I: Archaeological and Historical Results*, Berkeley, 1947
TN II	J. C. Wampler, *Tell en-Nasbeh II: The Pottery*, Berkeley, 1947
Water System	James B. Pritchard, *The Water System of Gibeon*, Philadelphia, 1961
Wirgin	Wolf Wirgin and S. Mandel, *The History of Coins and Symbols in Ancient Israel*, New York, 1958
Wroth	W. Wroth, *Catalogue of the Imperial Byzantine Coins*, London, 1908

THE WINERY

Among the principal results of the 1959 and 1960 seasons at el-Jib was the discovery of a large winery in Areas 8 and 17, within the northeast sector of the mound (Fig. 1). The evidence for the winery consists principally of storage cellars cut into the live rock of the hill and other smaller cuttings made for pressing the grapes and processing the wine. Although many of the facilities originally provided for the manufacture and storage of wine had been converted to other uses in subsequent periods, there was enough pottery within and around the cellars and other rock cuttings to provide evidence for the methods employed in the making of wine and for fixing the date for the last period of use for the winery.

Preliminary reports on the findings within Areas 8 and 17 have been published in *Expedition*, *The Bulletin of the University Museum of the University of Pennsylvania*, Vol. 2, No. 1, 1959, pp. 17-25; *BA*, Vol. 23, No. 1, pp. 23-29, and Vol. 24, No. 1, pp. 19-24; *The Illustrated London News*, Sept. 10, 1960, pp. 433-435; *BASOR*, No. 160, pp. 2-6 (inscribed jar handles from Area 8); James B. Pritchard, *Gibeon, Where the Sun Stood Still*, 1962, pp. 79-99.

In the following pages we shall first describe the cellars and other rock cuttings. The measurements of the cellars are given in tabular form (p. 3) and drawings of plans and sections are presented in Figs. 2-11. Descriptions of 36 of the most typical cellars are given in detail on pp. 2-8. Notes are also given on the stone covers for the cellars, the plaster found on the walls and floors of some of them, and on the other rock cuttings in the area. The debris found in the cellars is important for determining the date at which they ceased to be used for storage. In the second section of this study we have presented both the results of the day-by-day inspection of the pottery as it came from the excavation and detailed comments on the selected pottery and other artifacts which are published in drawing or photograph. Finally, we have sought to reconstruct the process of wine making as it can be determined from the evidence found at el-Jib.

THE ROCK-CUT CELLARS

The most obvious feature of the winery to have survived is the provision that had been made for the storage of wine at a constant temperature. Sixty-three jug-shaped cellars had been hewn from the live rock of the hill to a depth which averages 2.2 m. The opening at the top of these cuttings had been left small -- the average is 0.67 m. -- so that it could be closed conveniently with a relatively small slab of stone. After having cut the small opening at the top the quarriers had undercut the rock so as to form a cylinder, which averages 2 m. in diameter, and which has an average capacity of 1,500 U.S. gallons. Although there is considerable variation in size for the individual cellars, the plan is essentially the same.

Averages have been computed separately for Area 8 and Area 17 in the summary of measurements given below so that comparisons can be made between them. Although the average volume of the cellars in Area 17 is considerably larger than that of the cellars in Area 8, there appears to be no significant difference in the ratio of depth to diameter between the two areas.

1

AVERAGE MEASUREMENTS

	Area 8 (11 cellars)	Area 17 (42 cellars)	Total
Diameter of Opening	0.65 m.	0.67 m.	0.67 m.
Depth	2.0 m.	2.3 m.	2.2 m.
Diameter of Floor	1.9 m.	2.0 m.	2.0 m.
Volume	4.6 cu. m.	6.5 cu. m.	5.8 cu. m.
Capacity	ca. 1200 U.S. gal.	ca. 1700 U.S. gal.	ca. 1500 U.S. gal.

(Note: The figures for volume omit the volume of Loc. 208-209, which consisted originally of four cellars. Its volume, 23.0 cu. m., is approximately four times the volume of an average cellar. Its four openings are counted, however, in obtaining the average diameter for the opening; but Loci 137, 152, 215, and 217 are omitted in computing the average, since their openings are abnormally large and appear to be broken. In most cases, the floor diameter is slightly smaller than the maximum diameter of the cellar.)

DESCRIPTIONS OF CELLARS

Detailed descriptions are given below for 36 of the most important cellars. Some are included because they are considered typical; others, because they contained significant artifacts or exhibited structural features that offered clues for determining their original purpose or date of use. The walls of the cellars are without plaster unless otherwise noted. The debris which lay in the cellars was generally undifferentiated as to layers; but whenever the strata of deposits could be observed, mention is made of this phenomenon.

Loc. 103. The rim of the opening is broken except for a segment at the southwest. The floor is plastered at the west side, and there are traces of brown plaster on the wall at\ca. 1 m. below the opening and also at *ca.* 85 cm. above the floor. The debris consisted of loose dirt and a few stones. Several large, rough stones formed a curb around the opening. These stones were probably set in place when the cellar was reused as a cistern.

Loc. 104. The opening is slightly off center at the west. The chamber walls and floor are plastered with a gray, medium-fine plaster similar to that found on the curb above. The debris was not truly stratified but the following variations in the content of the layers were noted: down .40 to 1.50 m., miscellaneous rocks about 30 to 40 cm. in diameter, very little soil; down 1.50 to 1.60 m., soil, sherds, and very few stones; down 1.60 to 1.78 m., stones but very little pottery. A well-constructed stone curb, 1.20 m. high, is built on bedrock around the opening (Fig. 60). On top were two stones, *ca.* 50 cm. in length, that served as a cover for the cistern. The inner face of the curbing is plastered. The plaster does not penetrate between the stones; it appears only on the inside and outside of the inner row of stones. The outer row of stones in the curbing is set in dirt. In the process of dismantling the structure there were found tesserae, Byzantine sherds, and four reused grinding stones.

Loc. 105. The walls of the chamber and the floor were of harder limestone than those of Loc. 104. Five centimeters to the east of the opening is a circular cutting in the bedrock, measuring 22 cm. deep and 52 cm. in diameter; there is a slight depression in the

TABLE OF MEASUREMENTS

Locus Number	Diameter of Opening (meters)	Depth (meters)	Diameter of Floor (meters)	Volume (cubic meters)	Capacity (U.S. gallons)
103	0.76	2.3	1.8	5.0	1300
104	0.64	2.0	1.9	5.0	1300
105	0.92	1.9	2.0	4.8	1300
106	0.70	2.0	1.7	2.6	690
107	0.68	1.3	1.1	1.6	420
108	0.62	2.6	2.6	8.8	2300
109	0.64	2.3	2.0	5.1	1300
112	0.60	1.9	1.4	3.0	790
113	0.50	2.0	1.8	3.9	1100
114	0.60	2.3	2.0	6.2	1600
115	0.46	1.8	2.1	4.5	1200
135	0.66	2.7	2.0	8.6	2300
136	0.74	2.3	1.9	5.6	1500
137	1.46	2.8	2.0	7.5	2000
138 [1-6]					
139	0.70	2.6	2.5	7.3	1900
140	0.78	2.3	1.7	3.7	980
141	0.70	2.6	2.4	8.4	2200
142	0.64	2.3	1.5	4.9	1300
143	0.62	2.2	2.1	5.1	1300
144	0.70	2.1	2.2	6.3	1700
145	0.48	1.9	2.4	6.3	1700
146	0.74	3.2	2.1	9.7	2600
147	0.68	2.4	2.1	8.1	2100
148	0.44	2.3	2.0	5.6	1500
149	0.78	2.4	1.8	6.5	1700
150	0.74	2.6	2.0	6.2	1600
151	0.60	2.7	2.1	7.5	2000
152	1.16	2.3	1.6	4.2	1100
153	0.66	2.5	2.3	7.6	2000
154					
155	0.76	2.7	2.4	9.6	2500
200	0.76	3.0	2.1	9.7	2600
201	0.52	2.1	2.0	4.8	1300
202	0.84	1.9	1.8	3.8	1000
204	0.75	2.4	2.0	8.0	2100
208	0.58 ⎫				
208s	0.40 ⎬ 2.1		3.4	23.0	6100
209	0.88 ⎪				
209w	0.55 ⎭				
211	0.58	1.6	1.4	2.8	740
212	0.78	2.2	2.4	7.6	2000
213	0.72	2.4	2.4	7.2	1900
214	0.60	1.8	1.3	2.2	580
215	1.16	2.6	2.2	7.8	2100
216	0.82	3.1	3.5	23.0	6100
217	1.24	1.5	1.7	2.6	690
218	0.68	2.0	2.4	6.2	1600
219	0.70	1.9	1.6	3.1	820
221	0.90	2.5	2.1	7.6	2000
222	0.60	1.6	1.0	2.6	690
223	0.78	2.1	2.4	6.7	1800
224	0.54	1.7	1.6	3.2	840
225	0.68	1.8	1.8	4.7	1200
226	0.58	2.9	2.3	9.8	2600
227	0.80	3.0	2.2	9.4	2500
228	0.52	0.9	1.0	0.9	240
229	0.60	1.9	1.7	4.0	1100

(Note: Diameters of the openings are measured to the nearest centimeter; other measurements are approximations to the nearest 10 centimeters. Capacity is estimated generally to the nearest hundred gallons.)

rim of the cellar opening near the cutting (Figs. 57 and 58). The debris was not in layers, but it was noted that there was a coating of hard-packed soil and small sherds, about 15 to 20 cm. thick, near the walls; the debris in the center was loosely packed and contained only a few sherds. Near the bottom were four stones, averaging in size 20 by 25 by 5 cm., and one stone, 68 by 45 by 12 cm., leaning against the south wall. The cellar was tested for porosity (see below, p. 9).

Loc. 106. At the south side of the opening a circular stone wall of four courses built on bedrock serves to make level the rim of the opening to the cellar. At the north there are two courses of stone above the opening. Vertical and diagonal pick marks are visible on the walls. A shallow deposit of debris containing exclusively Iron II pottery suggests that the cellar was closed in the Iron II period. At 40 cm. above the floor at the south, there is a hole, 5 cm. in diameter, that extends for a distance of 1 m. into the rock; but no opening through the wall to the outside could be found. There was no stratification within the debris of soil mixed with a few stones.

Loc. 107. The opening is encircled by a wall built of three stones, which are about 20 cm. high, with smaller stones between them. On top were two flat stones covering the opening to the cellar. The opening is off center to the south. The debris consisted largely of damp soil; tesserae and fragments of glass were found near the surface of the debris. The walls and floor are fairly smooth; only a few pick marks are visible. One stone, 70 by 50 by 12 cm., near the floor may have been the original cover. The floor slopes toward the north.

Loc. 112. The walls and floor are very smooth. They are of a pinkish-tan color and there is no trace of plaster on them. The cellar was completely filled with debris. At 1.30 m. down, the soil was hard-packed along the sides of the wall. In the center the debris was mostly small stones. Below 1.45 m. there were many sherds and larger stones. At 30 cm. above the floor there were some clay and disintegrated pottery. On the south side, 15 cm. of the debris on the floor was damp, hard soil.

Loc. 135. This cellar has openings into Loc. 141 (75 by 46 cm.) and Loc. 142. The edges of the holes are smooth enough to have been cut intentionally. The east-west wall in 17-M-9 passes over part of the top opening but does not cut off access to the cellar. Two small, irregular depressions in the chamber wall at the south could have served as lamp sockets, although there is no trace of carbon deposit. Chamber wall and floor are relatively smooth and show very few pick marks.

Loc. 136. This cellar is connected with Loc. 147 and Loc. 140 by openings large enough to permit a person to pass through. Since the edges of these openings are smooth, the apertures were probably entrances rather than accidental breaks or holes in the walls. Some pick marks are visible at 50 cm. above the floor; the upper walls are smooth. Several large stones were found inside the cellar; some of them were large enough to have served as an original cover. There are some indications that the cellar may have had a secondary use shortly after the Iron II period--the pottery is reported as predominately Iron II. An adaptation, such as that suggested by the two openings in the walls, could explain the presence of two stamped *msh* jar handles that are dated to the 6th-5th centuries (Fig. 52:4,7). The debris was loosely packed to a depth of 1.96 m. The two stamped jar handles were found at a level of about 60 cm. below the surface of the debris.

Loc. 137. The cellar opening had deteriorated on the east side so that its original diameter can be estimated only on the basis of the arc preserved at the west. A channel in bedrock enters the opening at the north. The walls are fairly smooth near the tops. Some pick marks are visible near the floor. About 70 cm. down from the opening there is a small cutting in the wall large enough to have served as a lamp socket, but there is no deposit of carbon in or above it. It is near enough to the opening to have served as a step which could have been used by persons entering or leaving the cellar, although steps are not a regular feature of the cellars. The cellar was full of debris containing pottery that is exclusively Iron II. At the level of 1.29 m. below the surface of the debris a horizontal layer of hard-packed earth was noted.

Loc. 139. The chamber is flask-shaped, having a flat floor and walls sloping up to the mouth. The walls are comparatively smooth at the top. From a point about 1 m. above the floor and extending to it, the walls are marked by the sharp edges of the mason's pick. At about 20 cm. above the floor the debris was silt, and contained seeds, bits of charcoal, and decayed wood.

Loc. 140. This cellar is connected with Loc. 136 by an opening. The inverted slope of the west wall suggests that the cellar was quarried after Loc. 136 had been cut. The walls are comparatively smooth; very few pick marks are visible. About 1.10 m. down from the top at the northeast there is a lamp socket or small step. At some places on the walls there is a puzzling pinkish-tan color in the rock. A channel in the bedrock enters the top of the opening at the southwest, connecting it with Loc. 137. The wall near the center of 17-N-9 is built over the channel and is between the top openings of Loc. 140 and Loc. 137 (Fig. 61). A hard-packed earthen floor, about 10 cm. thick, was found near the base of the wall, but a relationship between the channel and the cellar openings could not be established. If the channel existed prior to the quarrying of the cellar, it must have been blocked when the cellar was in use; otherwise, waste water would have drained into the cellar. If the channel was cut after the cellar, it could have served as a drain into the cellar during the period of reuse.

Loc. 141. This cellar is connected with Loc. 135 by an opening in the common wall between them. Some pick marks are visible on the walls near the floor and also near the top opening at the west side; elsewhere the walls are smooth. A wall in 17-M-8 passes over the north edge of the top opening but leaves a space large enough for a person to enter. It was not possible to determine a chronological or functional relationship between this wall and the cellar. A cover, consisting of two stones large enough to cover the top opening, was found *in situ*.

Loc. 142. An opening in the wall connects this cellar and Loc. 135. The east wall slopes inward toward the bottom. Obviously the quarriers wished to avoid breaking through into the west wall of Loc. 141, which was cut earlier. There are traces of a pinkish-tan color in the rough or deteriorated rock of the walls at the south and southwest; elsewhere the walls are smooth and no pick marks are evident. There is a shallow niche cut into the wall at the east just below the top opening. The north-south wall in 17-M/N-8 passes directly over the top opening, but the lower courses of the wall are shaped so as to allow enough room for an entrance into the cellar. Five large stones, one of which is large enough to have served as a cover, were found inside.

Loc. 144. The walls of the chamber are irregularly cut. About 65 cm. below the opening there appear two roughly cut niches in the otherwise smooth surface of the walls. At 2 m. below the opening a layer of packed clay was noted. The pottery above and below this layer belongs to the Iron II period, except for a possible Iron I sherd from the debris below the clay level.

Loc. 149. There is a break-through into Loc. 153. In the walls there are two flaws in the rock, and two niches, one 80 cm. and the other 1 m. from the top opening. Pick marks on the surface of the walls are fairly prominent.

Loc. 151. The west wall has been cut away so as to make one large chamber with Loc. 150. To the south there is an opening into Loc. 155. Three lamp sockets (?) have been cut into the walls about two-thirds of the way up from the floor.

Loc. 153. A rough break, about 20 cm. in diameter, connects this cellar with Loc. 149. The walls are very rough; pick marks are prominent, in some places 3 cm. deep. The debris was mostly soil with very few stones. A cover, measuring 85 by 70 by 8 cm., was found *in situ.* There are three indentations in the floor near the center, the largest of which measures 16 cm. in diameter and 10 cm. deep. Four other cellars have cutting in the floor (Loc. 146 has a rough groove, about 75 cm. long and 12 cm. in diameter, in the floor near the east wall; Loc. 108 has a circular depression, measuring 80 cm. in diameter and 26 cm. deep; Loc. 113 has a small depression near the west wall; and Loc. 212 has a V-shaped depression in the center of the floor). It is possible that these cuttings served as settling basins, although they obviously were not considered essential features, since they are present in comparatively few cellars.

Loc. 155. This bottle-shaped cellar was entered by the excavators through the east side of the Roman tomb, Loc. 138. It is connected by a circular hole with Loc. 151. The top opening is covered by a single, round, flat stone, about 12 cm. thick. In the east wall, 1.21 m. below the top opening, there is a niche, 15 by 20 by 16 cm.

Loc. 201. The chamber is bell-shaped and the floor slopes slightly toward the center. Inside was found a round stone cover, measuring 50 cm. in diameter and 12 cm. thick, niched on one side by a groove that may have been used to engage the lever for raising the cover when it was fitted tightly into the beveled edges of the opening to the cellar.

Loc. 204. The lower part of the chamber is covered with a fairly coarse plaster that varies in thickness from 1 to 3 cm. The shape is normal and shows no evidence of modification such as that made in Loc. 138, which consisted of six cellars converted into a Roman tomb, or as in Loc. 225, 226, 227, which had been made into one large plastered cistern. It is not equipped with a curb as were Loc. 103 and Loc. 104, which had been plastered and reused as cisterns in the Byzantine period. From the presence of debris containing exclusively Iron II pottery for a depth of 1.10 m. above the floor it is clear that this plastered chamber must have been used in the Iron II period (the presence of a few Roman sherds on the top of this heavy deposit of Iron II debris indicates only that the cellar was open as late as the Roman period). Yet none of the cellars, with the exception of Loc. 208, 208s, 209, and 209w (to be discussed below), seem to have been plastered in the Iron II period of use. It is possible that in the process of making wine this rock-cut chamber served as a fermenting tank, where the freshly pressed juice was placed for a period of several days. This possibility is strengthened somewhat by the presence nearby of a system of basins, channel, and presses (Fig. 64), which may have served as a part of the installation for the manufacture of wine.

Loc. 208, 208s, 209, 209w. These four cellars formed a single chamber during the period of their final use and will be described together. So great was the modification of the original cuttings that it is now impossible to determine whether there were originally three or four cellars. The four openings suggest that originally there had been four; however, it is entirely possible that there were once only three cellars and that the fourth opening, Loc. 209, had been cut later. Other modifications which probably coincided with the cutting of the top opening, Loc. 209, included: (1) the blocking of top openings Loc. 208s and 209w; (2) the leveling of the surface above with *huwwar* and the building of a flagstone floor above the chambers in the vicinity of the openings, and the construction of a stone wall (Fig. 11) running north-south in 17-0-10/11 (the location of this wall was such as to place the openings of Loc. 209 and 208 in separate rooms); (3) the plastering of the cellar walls; and (4) the construction of a similar north-south stone wall on the floor of the cellar immediately below the wall on the ground level. A further modification was made when a tunnel was cut through the cellar wall at the north, connecting it with Loc. 211. The tunnel, measuring 55-60 cm. in diameter, is 1.15 m. above the floor of Loc. 208 (Fig. 68). On the northwest side of Loc. 209w there are niches which may have served as lamp sockets; two of them are *ca.* 1.10 m. above the floor, and one is 55 cm. above the floor level.

Loc. 211. Connecting this cellar with Loc. 208-209 is a tunnel, 1.10 m. in length, and measuring 46 by 34 cm. where it enters the wall of Loc. 211, 50 cm. above the floor. It seems likely that the tunnel was cut as a secondary feature. The top opening of the cellar was closed with a stone, over which passes an east-west wall of 17-0-11. Since the chamber is smaller than the average and the floor is uneven, it is possible that it was never completed as a cellar, or that it was used only during the earlier phase of Loc. 208-209. Afterwards it was abandoned and covered over, and a wall was built on top of the opening.

Loc. 212. An opening on the north side about 30 cm. above the floor, measuring 50 by 48 cm., connects this cellar with Loc. 213. The floor slopes toward the center to form a small basin.

Loc. 213. This cellar has an opening into Loc. 212 on the south side, approximately 20 cm. above the floor. The floor slopes slightly toward the center, as does the floor of Loc. 212, but is without a basin in the center.

Loc. 215. An opening, 50 by 30 cm., at the southwest side about 52 cm. above the floor, connects this cellar with Loc. 216. The top opening is unusually large and may have deteriorated or have been cut away after the abandonment of the chamber as a cellar. The floor slopes slightly toward the center.

Loc. 216. At the northeast side of this unusually large cellar there is an opening, measuring 50 by 30 cm., about 90 cm. above the floor, connecting it with Loc. 215. The floor is level and has a small basin cut in it at the west side. A rock cutting at the northwest of the top opening seems to have punctured the cellar in two places (Fig. 65). This accident seems to have been repaired by a large flat stone placed in the cutting.

Loc. 217. This cellar has a floor that slopes slightly toward the center. The top opening is larger than usual and appears to have deteriorated at the east. Four niches or slots in the rim at the west may have been made intentionally to hold the cover in place.

Loc. 218. An opening, 46 by 37 cm., at the east side connects this cellar with Loc. 229. The floor slopes slightly toward the center. A fragmentary stone wall in 17-0-6 runs between the openings of Loc. 218 and 217. Loc. 229, at the south, may be in the same enclosure as Loc. 218. The pottery on the bedrock as well as that in Loc. 218 was exclusively from the Iron II period.

Loc. 219. This cellar has an opening from the south side into Loc. 223, beginning about 20 cm. above the floor. The floor slopes toward the west, where there is a basin-like depression occupying about half the floor space. Two cuttings in the walls, one on the west side and the other on the north, could have served to hold lamps. The cellar was covered. A stone curbing was found in place (Fig. 63). Although there are walls east of Loc. 219, there is none in 17-N-11/12. Therefore, Loc. 219, 223, and 224 may have been located in an open courtyard. Although no clay floors could be traced within the area, there was some evidence that efforts had been made to produce a level area adjacent to the cellar openings by filling in with clay on the bedrock.

Loc. 223. This cellar is connected with Loc. 219 on the north side by an opening, 65 cm. in diameter, beginning 60 cm. above the floor. It is also connected at the west with Loc. 224 by an opening, measuring 60 by 78 cm., beginning 60 cm. above the floor.

Loc. 225, 226, 227. Three original cellars were joined together in the final period of their use. The interior walls of the original cuttings were close enough together so that they could be removed without too much effort to form a single chamber. The floors are level, but that of Loc. 225 is 1.10 m. above the elevation of the other two floors. In the period of their reuse the chambers and floors of all three cellars were plastered. At least two coats of plaster could be detected, one of rough plaster, 2 cm. thick, and the other of fine plaster, 1 cm. thick. The coating is remarkably well preserved over most of the walls and floors. Two stone covers, one set horizontally and the other vertically, were found in the opening of Loc. 225. There are stone curbings around the openings of Loc. 226 and 227. It is probable that those who plastered the chambers found it easier to build the curbs than to clear away the debris and cover the openings at the level of the bedrock. The quality of the plaster, the presence of exclusively Roman pottery in Loc. 225, 226, and 227, and the association of walls and floor levels in 17-P/Q-11 dating to the Roman period, make it clear that the modifications are Roman in date. Beneath fallen plaster in Loc. 225 there was found a layer of gray-black clay, 5 to 7 cm. thick. A deposit of the same type of clay was found on the plaster floors of Loc. 226 and 227, where the deposit was considerably deeper.

ROCK-CUTTINGS AT TELL EL-FÛL

Rock cuttings similar to cellars at el-Jib were discovered by W.F. Albright in 1933 at Tell el-Fûl (*AASOR*, Vol. 34-35, Pl. 29; see Pl. 13B for photograph and pp. 35-36 for discussion). Although these 14 cuttings are termed silos and cisterns in the publication the excavator has informed us that they were not plastered (letter of W.F. Albright, August 13, 1961). In computing the depth of these cuttings from the levels given on the plan of Pl. 29 we find that they vary in depth from 2.39 m. to 1.53 m., with an average depth of 1.82 m. The average depth of the cellars at el-Jib is 2.2 m. The openings at the top average about .55 m. in diameter, as compared to .67 m. for the average diameter of the openings to the cellars at el-Jib. The diameters of the bodies of the cuttings vary from 2.20 m. to 1.40 m., with the average diameter of 1.73 m. (the average at el-Jib is 2 m.). These measurements for the openings at the top and for the diameters of the bodies of the cuttings are only approximate, since they were measured from the reduced drawings in the publication. In addition to these 14 cuttings in the rock there are other smaller and more shallow basins that correspond to those found in the industrial areas at el-Jib. The dates assigned to the debris found in the rock cuttings at Tell el-Fûl extend from the 5th-4th century at the earliest to the time of Christ at the latest (*AASOR*, Vol. 34-35, p. 35, and the letter of W.F. Albright cited above).

COVERS FOR THE CELLARS

Only 4 cellars (Loc. 112, 137, 141, 149) were completely filled with debris; the others were filled to varying depths, as can be seen from the table of analysis of cellar contents (pp. 14-15). It is probable that originally all the cellars had been equipped with stone slabs to keep the warm air from the chamber as well as to eliminate a potential hazard in the courtyard where there were animals and children.

There were reported covers of stone from either within or over the following cellars: Loc. 104, 105, 106, 107, 108, 140, 141, 142, 153, 155, 200, 201, 202, 204, 208s, 209w, 211, 212, 213, 214, 215, 218, 219, 221, 222, 224, 225, 226, 227, 229. The following dimensions and descriptions may be considered typical:

Loc. 105, stone cover, 68 by 45 by 12 cm.

Loc. 107, stone cover, 70 by 50 by 12 cm.

Loc. 108, two stones, 30 by 30 by 60 cm. each.

Loc. 153, closely fitting stone cover, 85 by 70 by 8 cm.

Loc. 155, closely fitting cover, ca. 12 cm. thick, in place, viewed only from the bottom.

Loc. 200, fragments of stone cover, with grooves on one side, possibly for inserting lever (Fig. 69).

Loc. 201, round stone cover, 50 cm. in diameter and 12 cm. thick, with cutting for inserting lever

Loc. 208s, stone cover, 70 by 50 by 10 cm.; cellar opening niched to receive cover of 18 cm. thickness.

PLASTER USED IN THE CELLARS

The suspicion that the unplastered rock cellars were incapable of holding water or other liquids, such as oil or wine, was confirmed by an actual test of Loc. 105, an unplastered cellar which had limestone walls that appeared to be unbroken. As an experiment the cellar was filled with water to a point 58 cm. above the floor and observations of the depth of the water remaining were taken as follows on each of the four succeeding days:

First day at 10:20 A.M.	46 cm.
Second day at 10:30 A.M.	24 cm.
Third day at 1:30 P.M.	10 cm.
Fourth day at 8:00 A.M.	Empty

By far the greater number of the cellars showed no evidence of having been plastered. In Area 8 only 3 of the 11 cellars were coated with plaster; in each the plastering of walls can be attributed to a later modification. Loc. 109 was being used as a cistern by the landowner at the time of the excavations; Loc. 103 and Loc. 104 have curbings which can be dated to the Byzantine period by sherds found between the crevices of the stones; this reuse of the cellars as cisterns provides a likely occasion for the plastering.

In Area 17 there was no trace of plaster in 37 of the cellars. The following observations can be made about the plaster which was found in the following 15 examples:

Loc. 138[1-6]: Plastered in the process of converting these six cellars into a tomb of the Roman period (see below).

Loc. 148:   Modern plaster for conversion into a cistern used by the landowner.

Loc. 204.   Plastered with a coarse, grayish white mortar, 1 to 3 cm. thick, in the Iron II period.

Loc. 208, 208s, 209, 209w: Plastered in the Iron II period, after the walls which separated the chambers had been cut away and prior to the building of the masonry wall.

Loc. 225, 226, 227: Plastered in the Roman period after the walls that separated the three chambers had been removed to form a single, large cistern; the plaster was applied in two coats: one was a rough plaster, 2 cm. thick; the other a fine plaster, 1 cm. thick.

It must be concluded, therefore, that most of the cellars in Area 17, like those in Area 8, were not plastered when they were first used in the Iron II period and could not have contained a liquid. The obvious exceptions are Loc. 204, and Loc. 208, 208s, 209, 209w.

TYPES OF PLASTER

It is possible to distinguish three qualities or types of plaster applied to the walls and floors of the cellars.

(1) The plaster on the walls of Loc. 204 and Loc. 208, 208s, 209, 209w is generally thicker than that which coated the walls of cisterns plastered in the Roman or Byzantine period. An examination of samples from Loc. 208, 208s, 209, 209w reveals a poor quality of lime, a binder of hair or straw or some other organic material, and clay and finely crushed dark gray stone. There are no traces of crushed pottery. The plaster could have been hydraulic when applied, but when found it had disintegrated so that it was porous.

(2) Plaster samples from Loc. 225, 226, 227 appear to be composed of a high quality lime, crushed stone -- possibly basalt and sandstone -- and crushed pottery. It is a rather fine, white mortar sufficiently nonporous to be hydraulic. In appearance it is similar to a fragment found on the steps leading to the Roman tomb, Loc. 138.

(3) Samples from Loc. 103 and Loc. 104, both of which were used as cisterns in the Byzantine period, are gray in color, less porous than that from Loc. 204 and Loc. 208, 208s, 209, 209w, but not quite so hard as that from Loc. 225, 226, 227. The plaster contains some large pieces of white, chalky stone, and some gray and brown crushed stone; traces of charcoal are also present -- doubtless remains from the process of heating the native limestone to convert it into lime. There is no ground pottery in the plaster. It is possible that Loc. 111, about 5 m. southwest of Loc. 104, was a lime kiln where limestone was burned during the Byzantine period.

OTHER CUTTINGS IN THE ROCK

In addition to the cellars hewn from the solid rock of Areas 8 and 17 there are other shallow cuttings into the surface that are obviously associated with them. These are listed below by number, the area in which they are found, and the references to plan, section, and photograph.

The largest single group of rock cuttings is that of 9 shallow basins (Loc. 105a, 125, 126, 129, 130, 132, 133, 134, 205). Although these vary considerably in size and plan, each could have served as a treading basin for the pressing of the juice from grapes. To this group there may be added an unnumbered cutting northwest of Loc. 216 (Fig. 65), which may have been started as a tread basin but not completed because of an

TABLE OF LOCATIONS FOR ROCK CUTTINGS

Locus No.	Area	Figs.
105a	8-G-4	2, 4, 6, 58
110	8-G-5	2, 4, 6
111	8-E-3	2, 4, 6
125	8-E-3/4	2, 4, 6
126	8-E-4	2, 12
127	8-E-4	2, 12
128	8-E-4	2, 12
129	8-F-5	2, 12
130	8-H-5	2, 13
131	8-H-5	2, 13, 59
132	8-G-5	2, 13
133	8-F/G-4	2, 13
134	8-E-6	2, 13
205	17-M-10	3, 5, 8, 64
(at point 22)	17-M-10	3, 5, 8, 64, 66

accidental break-through into the roof of Loc. 216, a cellar below it. Loc. 129 is distinctive in that there is a smaller basin cut into the floor at the west that may have served as a settling or dripping basin.

Loc. 110 is difficult to classify. The diameter of the opening is larger (1.14 m.) than that of the average opening of the cellars and it is considerably deeper (1.40 m.) than the shallow basins. It is possible that the cutting was started as a cellar and then abandoned because of the difficulty of cutting flinty stone, which can be seen protruding from the walls.

Of special interest are the cuttings to the west and to the south of the mouth of the plastered cellar Loc. 204 (see Figs. 3 and 5, [17-M-10] for plans; and Fig. 64 for photograph). If, as we have suggested above, Loc. 205 is a basin for the pressing of grapes, then the liquid could be dipped from the wine press into a separation basin (points 10 and 11 in Fig. 3), from which the juice would flow into the plastered vat, Loc. 204. To the south of Loc. 204 there is a second basin (point 14 in Fig. 3), from which a liquid would flow by gravity into the twin basins at the south (Figs. 3 and 66). These basins are connected by an opening in the wall between them so that settlings would remain in the first basin as the clearer liquid overflowed into the other. Although the above reconstruction of the function of this system of basins and canals is highly tentative, it seems reasonably certain that the cuttings were made to channel and to contain a liquid.

The date for the last use of the smaller cuttings in the rock is even more difficult to fix than it was for the use of the cellars (see below). In Loc. 105a the pottery was predominantly from the Iron II period. The debris at the top of Loc. 110 consisted of *huwwar* chips without pottery; but from below 1.15 m. to the floor the pottery was exclusively of the Iron II period.

The rock cutting in Loc. 111 seems to have been modified considerably in the Byzantine period. The circular cutting was built up with stones and plastered (Fig. 2) so that it could be used as an oven or kiln. Quantities of Byzantine sherds and extensive deposits of carbon were found in the structure.

On the bedrock adjacent to Loc. 126, 127, and 128, the pottery was predominantly that of the Iron II Age; and Loc. 129 contained only Iron II pottery. On the bedrock adjacent to Loc. 130 the sherds were Early Bronze and Iron II, although those of the latter period predominate. Recorded from the bedrock adjacent to Loc. 132 were sherds of the Iron I and the Iron II periods, but in the south half of the square those of the Iron II period predominate. Adjacent to Loc. 133 the pottery was a mixture of Iron II, Iron I, and a few Early Bronze sherds. In Loc. 134 the pottery was Iron I and II. In 17-M-10, where the rock cuttings and the plastered vat Loc. 204 appear, the pottery was exclusively from the Iron II period.

In addition to the cuttings in the live rock of the hill there were several stone objects which had been carved from blocks of limestone. There are three stone mortars (Fig. 54), and a stone trough (Fig. 56) that may have been used for the transfer of liquids. Loc. 131 is a limestone block, roughly hewn on the bottom and sides (Fig. 59). The chamber inside is rounded on the bottom with sides that slope inward to an opening smaller than the diameter of the cutting. The opening is encircled by a shallow channel which is pierced vertically by a small hole leading into the chamber. A liquid poured into the groove around the rim would flow into the chamber through this hole. It is impossible to say what function this device performed, although it resembles in shape and size the "dye vats" found by Albright at Tell Beit Mirsim (*TBM III*, pp. 55-62, Pls. 51-53; cf. C. Kardana, "Dyeing and Weaving Works at Isthmia," *American Journal of Archaeology*, Vol. 65, 1961, pp. 261-266).

CONTENTS OF THE CELLARS

When excavations were begun in Areas 8 and 17 the cellars that we have described were either in use as modern cisterns or completely covered over with debris, which averaged about a meter in depth. The usual procedure of marking out plots, 5 by 5 m., and of leaving balks of 1 m. between the plot was followed. When the plot had been excavated to bedrock and the balks checked carefully for indications of floor levels, tip lines, significant changes in the color or the character of the fill, the balks which separated the plots were removed. In general it can be said that there was no evidence for any extensive occupation in the two areas of the cellars except that upon the bedrock itself. The fragments of walls found in the area of the cellars had been built upon the bedrock, which had served as a floor throughout the periods of their use. The debris which covered over the openings to the cellars, and which had in some instances filtered through the opening into the cellar itself, was not the accumulation from human occupation in the area of the winery; it had been washed down the hill from the higher occupation levels to the west. The tip lines, which one would normally expect to find in debris laid down by erosion, had evidently been destroyed by the cultivation to which this section of the tell had been subjected over a number of centuries. The undifferentiated thin layer of debris can be seen in Figs. 54 (left), 65, and 64.

Although there was in general no observable stratigraphy in the debris which overlaid the openings to the rock cuttings, there was a sequence of Byzantine, Roman, and Iron II pottery which could be noted from the examination of baskets of pottery from the upper to the lower levels. It seems likely that after the Iron II period of occupation on the higher level to the west there had been a gap in occupation, during which there was considerable wash of Iron II sherds over the area of the cellars. Similarly, debris from the subsequent periods of occupation had been washed down to cover the earlier deposit. Throughout the periods of the accumulation of debris cultivation had effaced the lines in which the debris had been laid down.

In this section of our report we are concerned with the debris that was found within the cellars and with the indications which this material gives for the history of their use. Obviously the pottery found within the cellars can provide no clues for the date at which they were cut; pottery and other artifacts may, however, provide a terminus for the last use of the cellars. Throughout the period of the original use of the cellars as storage places they would have been kept reasonably clean. Broken pottery which accumulated in them from season to season was probably removed from time to time. When they ceased to be used as storage chambers the debris, including broken pottery, would naturally fall into the chambers from the surface, provided they were not sealed by a covering stone. It is the first accumulation of pottery in the cellars that is most important. It provides a clue for either the last use of the cellar or the period immediately following its abandonment.

Here we shall consider the results of the day-by-day inspection of the pottery which was made by the director with the occasional help of a member of the staff. The data have been placed in tabular form. In the second column of the following chart there is a listing of the number of baskets of pottery from each locus. This is only a rough approximation of the quantity of the material, since no record was made as to whether the basket was full or only partly filled. In the third column the depth of debris is given, measured from the top of the filling within the cellar to the floor. The range of dates given in the fourth column is by general archaeological periods and indicates the earliest and the latest pottery. The assignment of periods makes no attempt to indicate the quantity of evidence, only the presence of one or more sherds that can be assigned unmistakably to the general period mentioned. The observations are based on field examination after the pottery had been cleaned but before it had been drawn. This record has value in that it was made when great quantities of sherds were available for observation and study. The analysis of pottery which was especially characteristic of cellars considered typical (see below) made in the final studies confirms the preliminary observations. In the fifth column there is a record of the depth of consistently Iron II pottery at the bottom of a cellar. Although the debris in the cellars was in no case stratified, a record was kept of the depths at which the baskets of pottery were found. In the final column there are references to the cellar descriptions (abbr. CD) given on pp. 2-8 and some additional observations on the cellars and their contents.

EVIDENCE FOR PERIODS OF USE

Of the 63 cellars that were discovered in Areas 8 and 17, only 52 contained pottery. Although no particular importance should be attached to the record of the quantity of pottery in either area or in the individual cellars within the areas, it is of interest to note that a total of 294 baskets was recorded. Of this number, 31 came from 10 cellars in Area 8 (omitting Loc. 109, in use as a modern cistern), and 263 baskets came from 42 cellars in Area 17 (omitting Loc. 138$^{1-6}$, reused as a Roman tomb; Loc. 148, in use as a modern cistern; Loc. 217, on which there is no data; Loc. 154, and Loc. 221, which produced no pottery). Thus, there were about twice as many baskets per cellar in Area 17 as in Area 8.

The pottery from the 52 cellars is chiefly from the Iron II period. It will be noted that 26 contained only Iron II pottery (Loc. 106, 113, 135, 136, 137, 139, 140, 142, 145, 149, 150,

TABLE OF DATABLE POTTERY

Locus Number	Number of Baskets	Depth of Debris (meters)	Range of Pottery Dates	Depth of Exclusively Iron II Pottery on Floor (meters)	Remarks
103	3	0.94	Byz.-Iron II	.57	See CD
104	3	1.35	Byz.-Iron II	.00	See CD
105	5	0.53	Byz.-Iron II	.25	See CD
106	2	0.41	Iron II	.41	See CD
107	1	0.30	Byz.-Iron I	.00	See CD
108	2	0.25	Iron II - Iron I	.00	Pit in floor; hole in east wall probably result of flaw in rock.
109	-	-	-	-	Modern cistern still in use.
112	8	1.65	Byz.-Iron II	1.15	See CD
113	2	0.43	Iron II	.43	Defect in floor at west; no evidence of reuse.
114	3	0.58	Iron II - Iron I	.00	1 MB sherd; a break at north opening into Loc. 115.
115	2	0.53	Iron II - Iron I	.00	Predominantly Iron II but some Iron I and MB sherd (tan, hand burnished).
135	15	0.74	Iron II	.40	See CD
136	6	1.96	Iron II	1.96	See CD
137	11	2.51	Iron II	2.51	See CD
138[1]					Loc. 138 is six cellars reused as a Roman tomb. As such the walls and floors were modified but the upper parts of the chamber, their openings and covers which serve as ceilings are preserved and recognizable as cellars of an earlier period.
138[2]					
138[3]					
138[4]					
138[5]					
138[6]					
139	6	0.53+	Iron II	.53+	See CD
140	4	2.08+	Iron II	2.08+	See CD
141	34	2.68	Rom.-Iron II	1.13	See CD
142	2	0.76	Iron II	.76	See CD
143	8	0.18+	Byz.-Iron I	.00	Break near floor opens into Roman tomb (Loc. 138).
144	9	0.88	Iron II - Iron I	.00	See CD
145	1	no data	Iron II	no data	Walls damp to 1 m. above floor; Iron II burnished ware, bowls, etc.
146	8	2.82	Byz.-Iron II	1.32	A rough groove in floor at east, ca. .75 m. long.
147	5	1.54	Byz.-Iron II	1.29	Break opens into Loc. 136; only 1 Byz. sherd in surface of debris; otherwise Iron II only.
148	-	-	-	-	Modern cistern still in use.
149	3	2.42	Iron II	2.42	See CD
150	9	no data	Iron II	no data	Wall with Loc. 151 partially cut out. Depth of debris and pottery not recorded.
151	15	1.80	Iron II - Iron I	1.45	See CD
152	6	1.94	Iron II - Iron I	.00	1 EB sherd intrusive in top 5 cm. of debris; Iron II - Iron I on floor.

TABLE OF DATABLE POTTERY (CONTINUED)

Locus Number	Number of Baskets	Depth of Debris (meters)	Range of Pottery Dates	Depth of Exclusively Iron II Pottery on Floor (meters)	Remarks
153	1	0.57	Iron II	no data	See CD
154	-	-	-	-	Opening visible from inside Loc. 138; no pottery; not cleared. Appears only on general plan of Area 17.
155	1	1.06	Iron II	1.06	See CD
200	6	1.00+	Byz.-Iron II	1.00+	Fragments of stone cover, on one side of which is a groove possibly for use with lever in raising the cover.
201	5	1.84	Rom.-Iron II	.64	See CD
202	5	1.72	Rom.	.00	Pottery is consistently Roman; two niches 1.20 m. above floor and on same level.
204	15	1.80	Rom.-Iron II	1.10	See CD
208	7	0.84+	Iron II	.24	See CD. Some Roman sherds detected in 1 basket 1.65 m. from top.
208s	1	0.84+	Iron II	.24	See Loc. 208 and CD.
209	8	no data	Iron II	no data	See CD; 1 MB sherd (herringbone incisions).
209w	1	-	Iron II	-	See Loc. 209 and CD
211	1	0.20	Iron II	.20	See CD
212	17	1.90	Byz.-Iron II	.55	See CD
213	8	0.80+	Iron II	.80+	See CD
214	2	0.50	Rom.-Iron II	.50	Not plastered but perhaps used in Roman period; Rom. sherds and Iron II (small amount) only.
215	7	1.55+	Iron II	1.55+	See CD
216	12	2.40+	Iron II	2.40+	See CD
217	4	no data	no data	no data	See CD
218	3	0.40+	Iron II	.40+	See CD
219	2	0.15+	Iron II	.15+	See CD
221	-	-	no pottery	-	Opening (doorway?) to Loc. 222; niche below rim of top opening; no pottery.
222	1	no data	Roman	no data	Opening (doorway?) to Loc. 221; small cellar perhaps not completed.
223	2	0.10+	Iron II	.10+	See CD
224	1	no data	Iron II	no data	
225	1	0.07	Roman	.00	Joined with Loc. 226, 227; see CD.
226	1	0.50	Roman	.00	Joined with Loc. 225, 227; see CD.
227	7	0.50	Roman	.00	Joined with Loc. 225, 226; see CD.
228	2	no data	Rom.-Iron II	no data	Pottery from floor only - Iron II; small cellar perhaps not completed.
229	-	no data	Iron II	no data	Entered from Loc. 218; sealed by stone cover, balk on top; pottery recorded with that from Loc. 218.

153, 155, 208, 208s, 209, 209w, 211, 213, 215, 216, 218, 219, 223, 224, 229) and that 11 more cellars (Loc. 103, 105, 112, 141, 146, 147, 200, 201, 204, 212, 214) had exclusively Iron II pottery in debris which varied in depth from .25 to 1.45 m. From 6 cellars which have Iron II pottery as the latest, there are recorded a few sherds from the Iron I period (Loc. 108, 114, 115, 144, 151, 152). Since there are no building levels within the winery area that can be attributed to the Iron I period, it seems likely that the Iron I sherds in these cellars are intrusive, having been washed down from the higher level of the mound. When these 6 cellars are added to the 37 cellars with exclusively Iron II pottery or with a consistent layer of Iron II pottery on the floor there are a total of 43 which bear evidence for having been last used in the Iron II period. There is no evidence to suggest that any of the cellars were reused after the end of the Iron II period, except those which were either plastered and reused as cisterns or reshaped as tombs in the Roman period.

The presence of only Iron II pottery in the debris or on the floors of 43 cellars can best be interpreted as indicating that when the original installation was abandoned in or immediately after the Iron II period, the pottery and debris gradually sifted into the cellars or was placed in them by those who leveled the area for use in connection with other structures nearby. Four of the cellars were full of debris (Loc. 112, 137, 141, 149), one of them being in Area 8 and the other three in Area 17. In addition, 15 contained a meter or more of debris (Loc. 104, 136, 140, 146, 147, 151, 152, 155, 200, 201, 202, 204, 212, 215, 216); the debris in the remaining cellars varied in depth from .94 to .07 m.

The case for placing the abandonment of the cellars either within or at the end of the Iron II period is strengthened by a further examination of the debris which is recorded from the 9 cellars which did not contain exclusively Iron II or earlier pottery or a considerable layer of this pottery on the floor. Of the 9, there were 3 (Loc. 104, 143, 228) which had in them some Iron II pottery. Of the other 6, there were 3 (Loc. 225, 226, 227) which were plastered as cisterns at a later period and contained only Roman pottery. These 3 cisterns are located in 17-Q-11/12 (Fig. 3), where the pottery and the walls near the mouths of the cellars indicate an extensive occupation in the Roman period. Obviously it was easier to clear out the cellars of the Iron II period and plaster them than to dig new cisterns. Of the 3 remaining cellars, Loc. 107 had only a .30 m. deposit of debris which contained glass and tesserae along with pottery of several periods, and there was evidence for a well-curb which had been constructed around the mouth of the opening; Loc. 222 is a shallow cutting, possibly an unfinished cellar which was cleared of its debris in the Roman period when a search was conducted for cellars which could be reused as cisterns; and Loc. 202, which contained exclusively Roman pottery, was probably cleared in the Roman period but found to be unsuitable for plastering because of the deterioration of the stone around the opening.

GENERAL PLAN OF THE WINERY

In the course of the excavations made in Areas 8 and 17 the full extent of the winery appears to have been exposed. As can be seen from Figs. 2 and 4, the 11 cellars and adjacent rock cuttings in Area 8 are clustered in a region extending approximately 15 m. from east to west and 10 m. from north to south. Since no cellars have been detected where the excavation has been completed to bedrock in the adjacent areas, it is likely that most of the installation has been discovered. There does not seem to be any pattern of arrangement to the cellars within Area 8, although 2 (Loc. 106, 109) are at the northeast, 4 (Loc. 103, 104, 105, 108) are at the east, and 5 (Loc. 107, 112, 113, 114, 115) are at the west. The fragmentary nature of the walls in these three places made it impossible to determine whether or not the cellars had been enclosed in rooms or court-yards. It does seem probable that the cellars were all cut at a time when the bedrock was exposed. Had new cellars been cut after debris had obscured the openings to older ones, there would have been the danger of breaking into adjoining chambers already in existence. The similarity in shape and size found in the cellars argues for their having been cut at the same period.

When we consider the cellars in Area 17 it is apparent that they are located in an area extending about 40 m. from north to south and 30 m. from east to west (Figs. 3 and 5). The areas to the east have been cleared to bedrock for a distance of 10 m. beyond Loc. 152 and 153 without detecting additional cellars. At the west, Loc. 201, 148, and 145 are near the limit of the excavated area. Similarly Loc. 138 and 229 at the south, and Loc. 219 at the north are located near the edges of the excavation in this area. Al-though it is possible that further excavations at the west, north, and south may reveal additional cellars, it is probable that the major portion of the installation has been cleared.

The walls in Area 17 are so fragmentary that their association with individual cel-lars cannot be established firmly. The presence of some fragmentary walls in the central region of the installation (17-N/O-8/9/10), where there was pottery of the Iron II period in the debris of the cellars and also at the base of the walls, suggests that there were house or courtyard walls contemporaneous with the use of the cellars. It is not possible to determine whether the cellar openings were in rooms or in open courtyards. Along the east (17-P/Q-8/9/10/11) and the south (17-N/O-6/7) sides of the installation, there are other fragmentary walls where the pottery in the debris at their adjacent cellars are datable to the Roman period.

It may be concluded that the period for the primary use of the cisterns in Area 17 was the Iron II period. After their abandonment, certain cellars (Loc. 138, 225, 226, 227) were used in the Roman period, and others (Loc. 141, 201, 202, 204, 214) were open as late as the Roman period; yet, in the absence of structural changes we cannot say that they were actually used in the Roman period.

SELECTED POTTERY AND OTHER ARTIFACTS

A selection of important or typical pottery and artifacts from the cellars is given in the photographs in Fig. 50 and in the drawings on Figs. 32-34. In the following list the illustrations are arranged according to the cellar from which they came.

Within Area 8, Loc. 112 is perhaps the most instructive when the debris which com-pletely filled it is considered. It has already been noted that there was pottery of the Byzantine period on the top of the debris which filled the chamber, but from an examina-tion of the pottery in the field it was observed that the debris to a depth of 1.15 on the floor contained only Iron II sherds. This judgment is confirmed by a further study of selected pieces from Loc. 112. Three storage jars (Fig. 32:3, 5; 33:11) and three small burnished bowls (Fig. 33: 1, 4, 5) were found in the lower 60 cm. of debris on the floor and the date of the earliest of these forms may serve as a terminus for the first use of the cellar. As suggested by the references given in the catalogue for these forms, an 8th-7th century date is probable. Similar ring-burnished bowls with thickened rims were

LIST OF POTTERY AND OTHER ARTIFACTS BY CELLARS

Locus Number	Fig. Number
103	32:7
104	32:1
106	33:25
112	32:3, 5; 33:1, 4, 5, 11, 21, 22
113	50:2
135	32:2, 9, 10, 11; 33:6, 14, 17, 18; 34:1, 4, 5
136	50:4, 7
137	33:9, 13, 16; 50:5
139	33:24; 34:14; 50:3
140	33:19
141	32:4, 6; 33:15; 34:3, 12
143	33:26
144	33:20, 30
149	50:6
153	32:8; 34:2
201	33:23; 50:1
208	33:29
211	34:13
212	33:7, 8, 12, 27
213	33:2, 3, 10
214	33:32
216	33:31
226	33:28, 33; 34:6, 7, 8, 9, 10, 11, 15

found at Gibeah in Fortress III, which had two phases, both dating to the 8th-7th century. Such a date is in accord with those assigned to similar bowls at Tell Beit Mirsim, Tell Qasile, Tell en-Nasbeh and other Palestinian sites. Storage jars of a type similar to those found in Loc. 112 have come from Level III at Lachish and from Periods VII and VIII at Samaria. At both of these sites the form appears to have been used mainly in the 7th century, although it may have continued in use during the 6th century.

The evidence for dating the primary use of the cellars is more complete for Area 17, where there are 18 cellars from which pottery and other objects are given in the illustrations. In general it may be said that the dating of the terminus of use in this area follows the same pattern as that suggested by the material from Loc. 112 discussed above. The period of primary use seems to have been the Iron II period; the few sherds of Iron I Age are obviously intrusive.

At least 5 cellars (Loc. 143, 146, 147, 200, 212) were open as late as the Byzantine period, although none of them was plastered and reused as a cistern. On the floors of 4 of these (Loc. 146, 147, 200, 212) there was Iron II pottery. Apparently the debris from the earliest abandonment was never cleaned from the chambers.

In Area 17, 6 cellars (Loc. 138[1, 2, 3, 4, 5, 6]) were converted into a Roman tomb and columbarium, and 3 cellars (Loc. 225, 226, 227) were joined, plastered, and reused as a cistern in the Roman period. In addition to the 9 cellars that were reused in the Roman period, 8 cellars (Loc. 141, 200, 201, 202, 204, 214, 222, 228) were open as late as the

Roman period. Comparatively thick deposits of consistently Iron II pottery on the floors of Loc. 141, 200, 201, 204 may have entered through the opening to the chamber shortly after the period of primary use. At any rate these cellars were not cleared after this material had been deposited and the debris from the Roman period accumulated on top of the earlier deposit. Other cellars, such as Loc. 202, 228, and 229, contained pottery which was consistently Roman in date, although there is no evidence for structural modifications into either tombs or cisterns.

As suggested by the listings in the table on pp. 14-15 the cellars in Area 17 which are most significant for dating the terminus of use in or at the end of the Iron II period are 18 cellars which had consistently Iron II pottery (Loc. 135, 136, 137, 139, 140, 142, 149, 150, 153, 155, 211, 213, 215, 216, 218, 219, 223, 224). Adding to this number the cellars that have an Iron II deposit on the floors, although open as late as the Byzantine period (Loc. 146, 147, 200, 212), and the ones also having an Iron II deposit on the floor, although open as late as the Roman period (Loc. 141, 201, 204), there are a total of 25 cellars which have material useful for determining a date for the terminus of the Iron II period of use.

Of this group special attention should be given to Loc. 135 and 153. The latter was sealed by a capstone, and Loc. 135 was obviously closed in some way, since the pottery in it, like that in Loc. 153, is consistently Iron II. Sherds of large storage jars came from Loc. 135 (Fig. 32: 2, 9, 10, 11), probably all of them from large four-handle jars of a common type. A complete jar of this type was also found in Loc. 153 (Fig. 32: 8). Parallels have been noted in the Catalogue to examples from Tell Beit Mirsim, Lachish, and Tell en-Nasbeh. Miss Tufnell notes, with reference to the Lachish examples, that comparative material is rare, but that evidence for the type at Tell en-Nasbeh may place them in the late 7th or early 6th century. Rims from other storage jars (Fig. 33: 14, 17, 18) found in Loc. 135 have their parallels from other sites, including Lachish, Tell Beit Mirsim, and Tell en-Nasbeh. In each case they are dated to the Iron II period, but it is uncertain as to whether they are early or late. Collared rims, such as Fig. 33:18, are generally dated earlier than those of Fig. 33:14, 17. A jar similar to Fig. 33:14 comes from Tell Beit Mirsim, where it is listed as from Stratum A_2 (7th century), although Albright noted related types that are earlier.

Fragments of 3 cooking pots (Fig. 34:1, 4, 5) were also found in Loc. 135. Although the diameter of the rim of Fig. 34:1 is smaller than that of the typical shallow type of cooking pot, and the diameters of the rims of Fig. 34:4, 5 are likewise only a little greater, we judge them to belong to the shallow type instead of to the smaller deep type with its distinctively profiled rim. According to the classification of cooking pots proposed by Aharoni and Amiran (*IEJ*, Vol. 8, 1958, pp. 174-175), who distinguish Early Shallow, Late Shallow, and Deep types, our examples appear to be of the Late Shallow type. At Hazor the transition between Early and Late Shallow types appears between Strata VIII and VII. In view of the fact that the Late Shallow type continues through Strata VII to IV at Hazor (9th-7th centuries), one may conclude that the cooking pots from Loc. 135 may also date from the middle to the end of the Iron II period. This conclusion is in accord with the evidence from Tell en-Nasbeh and Lachish, where the type was in use during the 7th century; at Samaria similar cooking pots were found in Period VII (7th-6th centuries); at Gibeah and Beth-zur cooking pots of this type were apparently in use as late as the Hellenistic period. One fragmentary cooking pot from Loc. 153 (Fig. 34:2) belongs to the Late Shallow type. Although the diameter of the rim is greater than that of the cooking pots from Loc. 135, it is still possible that it belongs to their period. One bowl from

Loc. 135 (Fig. 33:6) has parallels at Tell en-Nasbeh and at Tell Beit Mirsim and belongs to the type which continued in use as late as the 7th century.

On the basis of the parallels cited above it may be concluded that Loc. 135 and 153 were in use during the same period, and that, while this period seems to have been the 8th-7th centuries, it is possible that the cellars were open as late as the 6th-5th centuries.

In other cellars of Area 17 whose primary use was prior to the Roman period, the general chronological pattern of Loc. 135 and Loc. 153 is repeated, but with some exceptions.

From Loc. 136 come two stamped jar handles (Figs. 50:4 and 7). In both the reading is *m s h* and the stamps are on single-ridge handles near the top, where the handle joins the body of the jar. A similar stamped handle was found during an earlier season at el-Jib (*Hebrew Inscriptions*, p. 27), another came from the unstratified debris of a house area in 17-H-19, and others are known from various Palestinian sites (N. Avigad, *IEJ*, Vol. 8, 1958, pp. 113-119). Scholars are not agreed as to the date of this stamp, although there is a tendency at present to date it as post-exilic, from the 6th century to the Hellenistic period. Both stamps from Loc. 136 were found in the upper 65 cm. of the debris, and cannot be considered as evidence for dating the primary use of the cellar.

In Loc. 137 there was found a pair of tweezers (Fig. 50:5) which has parallels at Tell en-Nasbeh from loci dated in the 6th-5th centuries, and at Samaria from remains of the Herodian period (Roman I). Also from Loc. 137 comes a saucer-type lamp (Fig. 33:9) having a round base and flared rim; the type is often found with the high-footed lamp (see below, pottery from Loc. 212 and 213). The lamp would not be out of place in the 7th century, although the type was in use during most of the Iron II period. A jar fragment bearing a triangular impressed design (Fig. 33:13) differs in ware and form from the storage jars bearing a triangular impressed design (Fig. 32:7). A similar design appears on sherds from Gibeah, where they are judged to be from the 5th-4th centuries, and from Samaria, Period VII-VIII, where they are dated to the 7th century or later. A fragmentary funnel (Fig. 33:16) from Loc. 137 has parallels at Gezer and Tell en-Nasbeh (see Catalogue for references), but its date is uncertain.

From a point south of the top opening of Loc. 139 comes a stone seal (Fig. 50:3), which has no exact parallel, although the design is similar to those known from Gezer and elsewhere. Miss Edith Porada, who examined photographs of the seal and the impression, reported that it belongs to a type of Palestinian seal common in the 9th-8th centuries. From Loc. 139 comes a fragmentary decanter or bottle (Fig. 34:14). The closest parallels from Lachish are classified as Type J.8. Miss Tufnell observes that this type belongs with the latest groups from Lachish, their range being confined to the last years of the 7th and the first decades of the 6th century. In view of the fact that this vessel was found on the floor of Loc. 139 in *ca.* 50 cm. of debris, which was consistently Iron II, its date may have special significance as indicating the period of the primary use of the cellar.

From Loc. 140 comes a stopper (Fig. 33:19) which has a hole in the bottom and another through the sides, both opening into a small chamber in the lower half of the stopper. When it was in position in the mouth of a jar, the holes would have been below the jar rim and hence could not have been used for tying the stopper in place. The stopper was found *ca.* 1.50 m. below the top of the cellar, i.e. in debris *ca.* 80 cm. above the floor. The total deposit of debris contained consistently Iron II pottery to a depth of *ca.* 2.08 m.

In Loc. 141 there were rim and handle fragments of two jars (Fig. 32: 4, 6), one jar rim (Fig. 33:15), one cooking pot (Fig. 34: 3), and one juglet (Fig. 34:12). Although the cellar was full of debris (a depth of 2.68 m.) and was open as late as the Roman period, these pieces were found at several levels in the first meter of debris above the floor. One jar (Fig. 32:4) is ovoid in shape, and has two handles and a plain collar rim. Parallels come from Lachish, Level II, and from Samaria, Period VII (see Catalogue). Such jars date from the 8th-7th centuries, although they may have continued in vogue as late as the 6th century (cf. *TN* II p. 9, par. 40). No close parallels have been found for Fig. 32: 6; on the basis of a similarity to jar rims from Tell en-Nasbeh and Beth-zur it may be as late as the 5th-4th centuries. The collared rim (Fig. 33:15) would not be out of place in the 8th-7th centuries, although it may be slightly earlier than this period (cf. *AASOR*, Vol. 34-35, pp. 16 f.). The cooking pot (Fig. 34:3) is comparable to those found in Loc. 135 and 153 (Fig. 34: 1, 2, 4, 5) and with them may be judged as typical of the Late Shallow type of the 8th-7th centuries. The juglet (Fig. 34: 12) has no exact parallels, although it may be considered in connection with Lachish Type D.9. Of this type Miss Tufnell remarks that the shapes of the body vary in form, generally pear- or drop-shaped, having a flat disk base, carelessly attached handles and surfaces that are rather rough (*Lachish* III, p. 303 f.). Such juglets from Lachish are judged to be post-exilic. Similar types of juglet rims and handles from Tell en-Nasbeh are dated as Iron II, possibly continuing in use after 600 B.C. (*TN* II, p. 25, S 831-834).

From Loc. 144, down 1.40 m. from the top, i.e. in the debris *ca.* 70 cm. above the floor, comes a bronze fibula (Fig. 33:30). The clasp is fragmentary and the pin is broken. However, the fibula is complete enough to identify it with Type II from Tell en-Nasbeh and Type 2b from Lachish. At the former site, fibulae of the bow and two-piece coiled-spring type are mainly from the 7th-6th centuries, extending in a few cases into the 5th century. At Lachish, Type 2b appeared in Levels II and III, so that a date shortly before or after 600 B.C. would not be inappropriate for Fig. 33:30.

From Loc. 149 comes a molded horse's head, a fragment of a spout or a head of a theriomorphic or zoomorphic vessel (Fig. 50:6). Although the representation of the harness is not present, as it is in the examples from Tell en-Nasbeh, the designs of the head and mane are similar. Parallels summarized by Wampler suggest that such vessels were in use both in Iron I and II and as late as the 5th century (*TN* II, p. 52).

In Loc. 201 there were a bronze statuette of Osiris (Fig. 50:1) and a corroded iron blade with the rivet inserted through the blade; the rivet is fragmentary but protrudes on one side (Fig. 33:23). The depth of debris in Loc. 201 was 1.84 m. Although the pottery ranges from the Roman to the Iron II period, the presence of the statuette at a point 1.40 m. down from the top, i.e. *ca.* 70 cm. above the floor, suggests that it may belong to the period of the primary use of the cellar rather than to a later period. Similarly, the iron blade was found in the debris about 10 cm. above the floor. On the basis of parallels, the Osiris statuette may date to *ca.* 700-300 B.C. The iron blade is similar to the knives with straight back dated by Petrie to the late Iron Age (*Lachish* III, p. 387); in the absence of any distinctive characteristics, it is likely that the type was in use over a period of several centuries.

From Loc. 211 there comes a juglet with a round mouth. It has light, vertical burnishing and large white grits (Fig. 34:13). A deposit of 20 cm. of debris, in which the pottery was consistently Iron II on the floor, suggests that the cellar was closed after the period of its primary use. The juglet has parallels from Lachish, Samaria, and Tell en-Nasbeh (see Catalogue). Miss Tufnell presents a helpful summary of the comparative evidence and concludes that this type must have been in vogue during most of the Iron II period, but in some sites, such as Tell en-Nasbeh, it may have persisted as late as the 6th-5th centuries. Our juglet belongs to Lachish Type 292, i.e. Class D.5a and D.5b, which first appear in Level III (*Lachish* III, p. 296).

From Loc. 212 come two lamps (Fig. 33: 7, 8), a fragmentary rim of a hole-mouth jar (Fig. 33: 12), and one bronze spatula (Fig. 33: 27). Although the pottery from Loc. 212 ranges in date from Byzantine to Iron II, one of the lamps for which data is available (Fig. 33: 8), the jar rim, and the spatula were found in a context of debris containing exclusively Iron II pottery near the floor. As a result of considerable comparative study of high-footed lamps, beginning with Albright's discussion of the type from Tell Beit Mirsim (*TBM* I, p. 86 f.; III, p. 154), scholars have concluded that the type continued in vogue over several centuries, with greatest popularity in the 8th-6th centuries, but continuing into the 5th century. At Lachish such lamps are grouped with Class L.9-10, of which examples were found in Tomb 106 and in the buildings of Level II. Miss Tufnell observes that Class L.10 represents a late phase in the evolution of saucer lamps characteristic of the 7th century (*Lachish* III, p. 286). This is in accord with evidence from the East Jordan area and also from Tell en-Nasbeh (*TN* II, p. 46). For the same period at Hazor, a site in Northern Palestine, the high-footed lamp is not common, although this fact may have no significance as far as the el-Jib specimens are concerned. From Stratum V (Late Iron II) at Ramath Rahel is a high-footed lamp found with a round-base lamp and a hole-mouth jar (see Catalogue). Our specimen of the latter (Fig. 33:12) compares rather closely with Class I from Gibeah, for which Sinclair has published a helpful summary of the sequence from various Palestinian sites (*AASOR*, Vol. 34-35, pp. 31 ff.). Although certain types of hole-mouth jars continued in vogue as late as the Hellenistic period, it is probable that Fig. 33:12 dates from the 8th-7th centuries. The bronze spatula (Fig. 33: 27) is not so readily dated; on the basis of comparative studies made in connection with specimens from Tell en-Nasbeh, it was demonstrated that the type was in use as early as Iron I and as late as the Hellenistic period (see Catalogue). A similar spatula (Fig. 33:26) comes from Loc. 143, where there was a shallow deposit of mixed debris.

From Loc. 213, containing a deposit of 80 cm. of debris in which the pottery was exclusively Iron II, come two burnished bowls (Fig. 33:2,3), and one high-footed lamp (Fig. 33:10). As do the similar bowls and lamps described above, these suggest that the cellar was in use during the 8th-7th centuries, and possibly for some time during the 6th century.

The dates and even the functions of the following small objects are uncertain. Bone spatulas, polished on one or both sides, came from Loc. 144 (Fig. 33:20), Loc. 139 (Fig. 33:24), Loc. 106 (Fig. 33:25), Loc. 226 (Fig. 33:28) and Loc. 208 (Fig. 33:29). Since the pottery of Loc. 106, 144 and 208 is predominantly Iron II and that of Loc. 226 is exclusively from the Roman period, these bone spatulas may have been used over a long period, or must be considered as intrusive in Loc. 226. Parallels at Tell en-Nasbeh, Lachish, and Samaria are noted; in each case the date is uncertain, and the function is not clear, although they were probably used as pattern sticks in the process of weaving cloth (cf. *Lachish* III, p. 397) rather than as spatulas for applying cosmetics as has sometimes been suggested. A small iron cup (Fig. 33:32) comes from Loc. 214, where the debris contains pottery ranging from the Roman to the Iron II period. Two scrapers (Fig. 33:21,22) from Loc. 112 are associated with Iron II pottery and are from a cellar judged to have been used only during the primary period. They differ from spindle whorls in that they are larger, although they appear to have been shaped from pieces of pottery.

No exact parallels are known. They could have been used in the shaping of pottery vessels prior to firing, or in clearing sediment from jars that had been used for storage purposes. One bronze arrowhead (Fig. 33:31) comes from Loc. 216, but it is not of a type that can be classified as to date (cf. *Lachish* III, pp. 385 f.).

At this point we may summarize the evidence from the cellars in Area 17 for the period of their primary use. The likelihood, based on a survey of the evidence from a number of cellars, is that they, like those in Area 8, were used mainly in the 8th-7th centuries, and possibly as late as the 6th century.

Turning now to the question of the reuse of the cellars for other purposes in the Roman period, our best evidence comes from the material in Loc. 225, 226, 227. These were cleared of earlier debris in the Roman period, modified in structure so as to make one chamber, plastered, and equipped with stone curbings at the two openings lying to the north. From Loc. 226 come three ribbed cooking pots (Fig. 34: 6, 7,8), three ribbed jugs (Fig. 34: 9, 10, 11) and one lime-stone cup (Fig. 34: 15). The cooking pots are of a fairly common type judged to be early Roman or Herodian, and are known from Herodian Jericho, Samaria (Roman level 3a), and elsewhere (see Catalogue). Close parallels for the cooking pots and the juglets also come from Stratum IV (Roman) at Ramath Rahel (see Catalogue). The limestone cup may also be early Roman as judged by parallels from Herodian Jericho and Cave 1 at Murabbaᶜat. It seems likely that Loc. 225, 226, 227 was used as a cistern in the 1st or early 2nd century A.D. A limestone stopper (Fig. 33:33) also comes from Loc. 226 but parallels have not been noted.

Although there is no reason for concluding that each cellar in Areas 8 and 17 followed a chronological pattern identical to the ones described above, the following sequence seems to be justified by the evidence: (1) there was a use and probably reuse of the chambers as cellars in the 8th-7th centuries, possibly continuing into the 6th century; (2) the installations were abandoned until the Roman period when some were used as tombs and others as cisterns; (3) after another period of abandonment, some were used as cisterns in the Byzantine period.

COINS

A total of 19 coins was found in those regions of Area 8 and 17 where the cellars are located. Of this number, 3 were found in the cellars, the others in the debris above and in the vicinity of the openings. The 3 coins from the cellars are as follows: C69, Alexander Jannaeus type, in Loc. 201, down 1.30 m. from opening; C75, Procurator Pontius Pilate, in Loc. 208; C77, Procurator Antonius Felix, in Loc. 214, down 1.65 m. Each of these cellars was found to contain some Roman type pottery and is judged to have been open as late as the Roman period, although not cleared and reused as a cistern or tomb.

Five coins come from Loc. 203, a room in 17-P-10 where Loc. 214 (see above) is located. The room is dated in the Roman period. The coins are: C73 and C72, Herod Agrippa I, down 1.20 m. and 1.90 m.; C70, Procurator Antonius Felix, down 1.65 m.; C71, Ptolemaic, probably Tyre, 1st century B.C., down 1.20 m.; C74, unidentified, down 1.90 m.

Three coins come from Area 8, although none is from a cellar. They are: C52, Constantius II (?), 8-F-4, down 1.15 m.; C56, Heraclius, 8-D-4, down 40 cm.; C51, Herod I, 8-F-4, down 1.15 m. on east side. Of the preceding, the first comes from the area between Loc. 103 and Loc. 104 which is judged, on the basis of pottery and construction, to have been reused in the Byzantine period. Similarly, the second was in the debris associated with Loc. 111, a Byzantine oven or kiln. The third may be considered intrusive since there are no Roman structures in the area.

Six coins come from 17-P-11/12, where the house walls are judged to be Roman and where the cellars, Loc. 225, 226, 227, were plastered and reused in the Roman period. Only two of the coins can be attributed with certainty. They are C79, Herod Agrippa I, down 1.60 m. below floor, and C86, Herod Agrippa I, down 2.20 m., north of oven.

One coin, C76, Herod Agrippa I, down 70 cm., is from 17-O-7, which contains walls judged to be Roman; there are no cellars near the walls. One coin, C55, Ptolemaic (?), down 20 cm. in 17-M-9, is so near the surface as to be considered intrusive.

In summary, the provenience and dates of the coins are in accord with the conclusions reached concerning the reuse of certain cellars in the Byzantine and Roman periods, as judged by the pottery sequence of the debris in the cellars, by the structural modifications of the cellars, and by the date of the buildings associated with the reused cellars.

INTERPRETATIONS AND CONCLUSIONS

Before the beginning of the 1959 excavation, when the industrial installations in Areas 8 and 17 were discovered, there had already been found in the great pool evidence for winemaking at el-Jib. It consisted of 56 inscribed handles which seemed at the time of their publication (*Hebrew Inscriptions*; Introduction dated July 12, 1958) to have come from wine jars, a clay funnel, and more than 40 clay stoppers which must have been intended for the wine jars found in the same context of debris within the pool (*Hebrew Inscriptions*, p. 16). It is not necessary to repeat here the arguments presented in 1958 for the existence of a winery somewhere in the vicinity of the pool; it should be pointed out, however, that on the basis of artifacts discovered during the first two seasons, it was possible to conclude that "the debris in the pool was from an area of the town in which the wine was made and bottled or from a storehouse where the empty jars were returned and stored after their contents had been consumed in neighboring towns" (*Hebrew Inscriptions*, p. 17).

In the following season of 1959 this guess that the source for the inscribed jar handles, funnel, and stoppers was near the pool was rendered more probable by the discovery of four more inscribed jar handles within the debris which overlaid the bedrock of the industrial area in Area 8 (*BASOR*, No. 160, pp. 2-6). Although none of these additonal jar handles came from stratified debris, their presence within the thin layer of soil which overlay the rock cuttings in Area 8 would seem to suggest that the contents of the pool, including as it did the 56 inscribed jar handles, had either been washed or filled in from the higher area to the northwest which produced the 4 additional specimens of the same type of inscribed handles. Thus, even before the cellars and other rock cuttings were discovered there was some circumstantial evidence for the existence of a winery at el-Jib and this circumstantial evidence was connected through the discovery of the additional jar handles in 1959 with the very section of the tell where the enigmatic cuttings in the rock first appeared.

The 63 cellars cut into the bedrock of the fill in Areas 8 and 17 are unique, except for the possible parallel to the "cisterns" discovered by Albright at Tell el-Fûl (p. 8). They were obviously intended for the storage of some commodity in large quantity.

Cereals can be eliminated as a possibility for two reasons: first, the damp walls and floors of the cutting would probably induce mildew on the grain; and secondly, the threshing area of the city was most likely on the western side of the hill, where there is generally a prevailing breeze. The possibility that the cuttings were cisterns for containing water is ruled out by the general absence of plaster on the surfaces of the porous limestone walls. There remain only the two possibilities of oil and wine as products which could have been stored in the cellars.

Since it has been impossible to detect any traces of either of these two volatile products on the walls of the cellars or on the jars found in them, the choice between them must be made on grounds of probability. The more convincing reasons for the choice of wine as the product made in the industrial areas and stored in the cellars are the following:

(1) The inscribed jar handles found in Area 8 and within the great pool seem most likely to have been labels for wine (*Hebrew Inscriptions*, p. 16).

(2) The extensive facilities for storage, 63 cellars, each with an average capacity of *ca.* 1500 U.S. gallons, would appear to be too large for the amount of oil which would normally be produced in a village the size of Gibeon. Wine, which was certainly consumed in greater bulk than was oil, would seem to be the more likely product requiring such extensive facilities. It might also be argued that the requirement for a constant temperature control, such as that provided by the rock-cut cellars, is more necessary in the production of wine than it is for the storage of oil.

(3) The facilities for pressing, in the form of tread basins cut into the rock adjoining the cellars, are better suited for getting the juice from grapes than they are for extracting the oil from olives.

RECONSTRUCTION OF THE PROCESS OF MAKING WINE

A provisional reconstruction of the process of making wine at Gibeon follows. When the grapes had been pressed by the feet of the treaders in basins, such as Loc. 129 and Loc. 205, both of which would have accommodated two people easily, the juice, skins, stems, and seeds were dipped out into intermediate basins, where as much of the solid matter as possible was separated from the juice. The juice was then transferred to a fermenting tank, such as the plastered Loc. 204, where the initial fermentation took place. If we are correct in our interpretation of the cuttings to the south of Loc. 204 as filtering basins, then the partly fermented juice was further refined of solid matter in a process of decanting before it was poured into the storage jars.

The one complete storage jar found in the cellars is that shown in Fig. 32:8 (P1106) found lying in loose soil near the floor of Loc. 153. Its capacity is 9¾ U.S. gallons. Although this was the only complete specimen of a storage jar found in the cellars, there are many fragments of a similar type of jar found in Loc. 135, and it is reasonable to suppose that this four-handle storage jar was generally used for the storage of wine within the cellars. These jars could be lowered through the narrow mouth and stacked in rows around the cylindrical chamber (Fig. 52). The height of the average cellar would easily accommodate two layers of the stacked jars (Fig. 53). On the basis of a conservative estimate the 63 cellars could have accommodated enough jars to store in excess of 25,000 gallons of wine.

The cellars are cut to a depth which is convenient for the process of filling and emptying them. It is possible for a man of average height, while standing on the floor and without using a ladder, to lift a heavy jar from inside the average sized vat to a position from which it can be taken by another who stands above the opening on the outside. The average diameter of 2 m. was probably determined by the extent to which the rock around the mouth could be undercut without weakening the rock which served as a roof. The openings, which averaged 67 cm. in diameter, were made large enough to admit a man, but were kept purposely small so that they might be covered easily by a flat slab of stone.

When the jars of wine had been placed in the cellars and the opening covered with a stone slab or with a bevelled stopper, the temperature would be kept fairly constant throughout the fall and winter months. On June 18, 1959, when the temperature registered 83.5° Fahrenheit in the shade, the temperature of water in the rock-cut cistern Loc. 109 nearby was 65°. It is of interest to note that in the winery of the Trappist Monastery at Latrun, some 13 miles to the west of el-Jib, wine is stored today in rock-cut cellars where the temperature is approximately the same as that in the cellars at el-Jib.

How long wine was generally kept in the cellars cannot be determined. They did provide, certainly, the best and the only means of refrigeration or temperature control at a fairly constant level.

When the wine had aged properly the large storage jars were removed from the cellars and the contents either consumed or transferred to smaller jars for shipment to neighboring cities. We do not have a complete jar with inscribed handles, but the best preserved of them indicates a jar considerably smaller than the storage jar found in Loc. 153. The making of an air-tight seal for the wine can be done by the use of a small amount of olive oil floated on the top of the surface of the wine in the jar. We do know that the smaller containers with the inscribed handles had stoppers of clay which were probably held firmly in place by a string placed through the two handles of the jar and then crossed on the top. The olive oil floating on top of the surface of the wine would have provided a seal and the stopper set, perhaps in clay or bitumen, and secured by the string above it, would have prevented the loss of the wine during transport.

To this reconstruction of the process of making and bottling of wine made on the basis of a suggested use of the installations and artifacts found during the course of excavation, there may be added certain clues derived from literary references found in the Bible. According to Isa. 5:2, wine presses were hewn out of the rock and grapes were pressed by foot in such a way that the garments of the treaders were often dyed red from the juice as it splashed upon them (Isa. 63:3). The crushing season was a time of joy and singing, and the treading was usually done with two or more people in the wine press (Jer. 48:33). In a list of government officials during the reign of David there is an entry which mentions the royal wine cellars: "and over the produce of the vineyards for the wine cellars was Zabdi the Shiphmite" (I Chron. 27:27).

A graphic representation of the process of making wine is to be found in the wall painting on the tomb of Nakht at Thebes (Norman de G. Davies, *The Tomb of Nakht at Thebes*, 1917, Pl. 23b, 26, pp. 69-70). This painting, dating to the end of the reign of Amen-hotep II or to the early years of Thut-mose IV, shows two men gathering grapes from vines trained in the form of an arbor. To the left, five men tread out the grapes in a covered vat, as they hold on to straps attached to the roof. The juice flows into a container to the right of the vat, and an attendant stores it in jars with large stoppers (shown stacked above). In addition to this painting there is a bas-relief on stone from the tomb of Mereru-ka (6th dynasty, 2350-2200 B.C.) at Sakkarah which depicts two musicians beating time to set the pace for those who tread the wine press (The Sakkarah Expedition,

The Mastaba of Mereruka, Pt. 2, 1938, Pl. 114).

In view of the magnitude of the installations at Gibeon for making and storing wine it is likely that the grape harvest season was a public festival, as it is known to have been from the reference in Jer. 48:33. If it was an occasion for celebration, then the open spaces which appear around a cluster of cellars in Area 8 and to the northwest of the winery area in Area 17 would have provided room for a large number of participants. It is also possible that these open places were utilized for the storing of grapes when they were brought in for pressing at the harvest time.

Two minor clues for the wine industry at Gibeon, while not in themselves conclusive, are worth pointing out as supporting evidence for the hypothesis we have set forth. One is the mention of "wine-skins" which the Gibeonites carried on their visit to Joshua at Gilgal (Jos. 9:4). One can only ask if it may not be possible that imbedded in the ancient tradition about the Gibeonites is the mention of a feature of the economic life of the city, that of a thriving industry in the manufacture and export of wine? The other clue is the observation that today grapes grow as one of the principal crops of the inhabitants of el-Jib.

Without samples of actual residue of the product which was stored in the jars placed in the cellars at Gibeon it is impossible to state categorically what it was. By a process of elimination of the various possibilities we have set up a working hypothesis that the rock-cut installation was for the purpose of making and storing wine. The facts recovered during the excavation of the areas during the seasons of 1959 and 1960 seem to be best explained by this hypothesis. Thus there remains a high degree of probability that sometime toward the end of the 7th century or the beginning of the 6th an extensive winery was destroyed or was abandoned. Some of its cellars, cut with so much hard labor, were to be used later for tombs, pits for refuse, and for cisterns, but never again was the elaborate industrial installation to be the scene of winemaking as it had been in the earlier centuries of the life of Gibeon.

ROMAN TOMB AND COLUMBARIUM

A major reuse of six wine cellars in Area 17 (Loc. 138) was their adaptation into a tomb and a columbarium (Figs. 14-16). The conversion of rock cuttings originally designed for the storage of wine into funerary chambers was accomplished by (a) cutting away the rock which separated them so as to make a large underground room, (b) cementing over the original openings at the top, and (c) cutting a stairway and door to the tomb. It is evident from the curbs of stone built around the original openings to the wine cellars (Fig. 15B) that at the time of the conversion into a tomb the bedrock was covered over with a layer of debris, possibly a meter deep. The well-built stone curb had been covered over with large stones and sealed with hard cement (Fig. 73). It was through one of these openings that an entrance had been made into the tomb in recent times; subsequently the landowner had partly filled the tomb chamber with field stones through this opening.

The adaptation of the cellars to funerary uses was not made at one time. The latest use of the tomb for burials is indicated by the discovery of 15 lamps (Fig. 49A) which were found scattered about the floor of the tomb (see below), and some guesses may be made about dates for the several periods of construction from the general plan and from the decoration on the walls. Since the tomb had been robbed in ancient and in modern times and its walls defaced by iconoclasts and vandals it is difficult to do more than place the construction and uses of the tomb within general limits.

DESCRIPTION OF THE TOMB

The entranceway to the tomb consists of a stairway of 12 steps cut from the rock for a length of 10.70 m. The orientation of the stairway is slightly to the north of northwest-southeast. It appears in one of the few possible places in the industrial installation of Area 17 where there were no wine cellars cut in the earlier periods; the tomb proper, however, not only makes use of the four wine cellars but appears in an area which was honeycombed with these cuttings. The placing of the entrance to the tomb in one of the few places in the areas where there are no wine cellars might suggest that its orientation was a matter of practical consideration. The walls of the entranceway would have been marred had it been cut in an area where there were earlier cellars. The sides of the stairway are plastered. The edges of the cutting for the stairway are lined by a stone wall of two courses (see section, Fig. 15 and plan, Fig. 3). The wall continued across the south end of the cutting for the stairs and was probably plastered over in one continuous surface with the wall formed by the rock of the cutting. It is not unlikely that this stairway was once covered over, but no traces of a covering remained. Had it been left open, surface water in the rainy season would have collected in it and could have filtered into the tomb.

DOORWAY

The doorway to the tomb, measuring 69 by 95 cm., consists of well-dressed stone built into the opening cut in the live rock (Fig. 76). The door itself (Fig. 79) was found lying on the floor inside the tomb. It is of a single slab of stone, 83 by 103 cm., of the same good quality as that of the facade. It had originally swung on projections which fitted into two sockets, one at the top and one at the bottom on the west side of the doorway. A notch for a bar by which it had once been secured in place appears on the east side of the doorway (Fig. 76), but the method for bolting it could not be determined. Inside the doorway there is a passageway, 1.07 m. long, which widens slightly toward the interior. Three shallow steps lead down to the floor of the tomb, where the final step, 90 cm. wide by 40 cm. deep by 45 cm. high, has been left in the live rock of the floor.

THE TOMB

The plan of the oblong chamber, tapering toward the south, seems to have been determined by the positions of the chambers of the four cellars of which it is obviously an enlargement (see dotted lines of the upper openings and shoulders of the four cellars in Fig. 14). The curved surfaces of the walls of the two cellars at the north are still apparent in the walls of the tomb at that end. On the west side of the tomb, 7 loculi appear in the floor (see Figs. 14 and 15) side by side, oriented approximately east-west; 3 more had been cut on the east side of the floor of the chamber oriented approximately north-south; and one additional loculus appears in the remaining space in the floor at the south of the tomb. The dimensions of the 11 loculi differ slightly; the average is somewhat over 2 m. in length, 1 m. in depth, and 60 cm. in width. From the spacing and the similarity in size it seems that these burial vaults were cut at about the same time according to one general plan of construction. The entire area of the loculi was floored with limestone slabs, with an approximate size of 1 m. by 45 cm. by 25 cm. In quality of stone they resemble the live rock from which the tomb was cut, and it may well be that they were quarried when the tomb was hewn. As can be seen from Fig. 14, the slabs covered only the loculi; there were no slabs in the path from the doorway to the back of the tomb chamber. The slabs over the loculi were covered over with a thick layer of plaster. All the loculi had been robbed of their principal contents; all that could be salvaged from them were lamps (discussed below) and a piece of sheet lead, measuring 9 by 12 cm., which had once belonged to a coffin.

The surface of the walls of the tomb exhibits the long vertical strokes of a flat blade. Two layers of plaster still adhered to the walls in places. The first is a heavy layer of gray cement, which was chipped while still damp to provide a rough surface to which the overcoat could adhere. A thin coat of white plaster, 0.5 cm. thick, had been placed over the cement. The ceiling also had been given a similar treatment of two coats. Since the plaster on the walls did not extend below the tops of the covers for the loculi, it is apparent that the cutting of the loculi had preceded the plastering or that the plastering had been done as a part of the same operation as the cutting of the loculi.

A secondary provision for burials is to be seen in the arcosolia cut in the walls of the tomb chamber. Four of these, two at the north and two at the south (Fig. 14), had been completed and apparently used. Two others on the east wall of the tomb had been marked out and begun, but never completed because of the discovery of wine cellars just behind the wall (Fig. 74). Another on the west wall, just back of the columbarium, seems to have been begun, but work was abandoned on it when an opening was broken through into the columbarium behind (see section, Fig. 15 for break-through into columbarium). The arcosolia were cut, apparently (see Fig. 74) after the mural (described below) was painted.

MURAL DECORATION

Around the walls of the tomb was a mural of paint and applied stucco work, about 65 cm. wide, extending from the ceiling downward to about eye-level. The plastered wall had first been primed by the application of a beige wash and coated with a dark blue wash. Although most of the plaster from the ceiling had fallen, a few remaining patches made it clear that the ceiling had been subjected to the same treatment as the walls. The central designs of the mural had then been outlined and the stucco bas-reliefs applied to the painted wall. The stucco work was held in place either by blobs of stucco, applied like dabs of paste, or by nails of iron inserted at intervals (Fig. 74, upper right, for four nails which held plaster figure of human form). After the applied work was in place, part of the background seems to have been given another coat of dark blue paint to cover the joins of the stucco and the painted wall. Long curling ribands of white (now somewhat bluish in color) had been painted into the background and made to appear as though they were tied to the garlands. Finally, touches of yellow, in imitation of gold, paint had been added to the ribands at points. Extending completely around the chamber, except for its interruption at the doorway and on the small wall immediately to the left of the entrance, there was a molded egg-and-dart border (Fig. 74).

The design of the mural is repetitive, but the elements which are repeated in the frieze are nowhere completely preserved. The entire decoration has, however, been satisfactorily reconstructed by Robert H. Smith. Photographs were taken of the entire east and south walls of the tomb and enlargements to the same scale were pasted together in one long strip. A celluloid sheet was placed over the photographs and the sure details in each repeated panel traced upon the overlay. By moving the celluloid sheet from one panel to another it was possible to utilize the details remaining in one panel to reconstruct those which were missing in another. The result of this careful reconstruction is shown in Fig. 17. The only detail appearing on the reconstruction for which there is no evidence in the photographs is the detail on the faces of the gorgonea and the genii, this conjectural reconstruction rests solely on parallels found in similar representations elsewhere. (There is also no clear evidence for the position of the hands, although the arms are well indicated. The sex of the genii is assumed to be male on the basis of the body structure and of the motif involved.) The garland at the extreme left of the panel is considerably shorter than the standard types found elsewhere and there is no space for the right arm of the genius to the right of this garland. This contraction of the usual proportions for the repetitive design is most likely due to the limitation of space which the artist found at the corner of the room. He had apparently started his mural at the west end of the south wall and worked around to the doorway. The actual photographs of the walls on which the mural appears are seen in Figs. 74, 75, and 76, with the most significant details shown in Figs. 77 and 78.

DETAILS OF THE FRIEZE

The principal features of the design on the frieze are (1) winged figures of genii, (2) garlands decorated with ribands, and (3) oval medallions, probably of gorgonea. The major elements of the frieze, the genii, garlands, and medallions were of fine, white plaster, probably cast in molds and then attached to the wall by means of square iron nails for the heavier pieces and with blobs of plaster for the lighter elements of garlands. In no place did an example of the applied plaster decoration survive the mutilation of vandals or iconoclasts. Fragments of the stucco work however, adhered to the wall and made it possible to recover the outline of the figures. Nails and nail holes still visible in the wall were a further aid in the reconstruction. Minor elements such as the wings of the genii, the ribands, and a fringe for the garlands were painted directly on the wall with paint in white and golden yellow.

The decoration on the walls of the tomb is unique for Palestine, although certain elements within it are to be seen in the painting on the Marwa tomb in Transjordan (*QDAP*, Vol. 9, pp. 1-30, Pl. 1).

THE COLUMBARIUM

To the west of the tomb is a columbarium (Fig. 14) which has been constructed from two wine cellars (see Fig. 80 for a photograph of the inside of the neck of one of the cellars converted into a columbarium). It is probable that the original entrance into the columbarium was from the south, an area which we were unable to excavate because of a valuable fig tree growing there. There are approximately 200 niches carved in the west, north and east walls of the columbarium. The average measurements are 20 cm. high by 30 cm. wide by 20 cm. deep (Fig. 81).

There is some indication that the columbarium is older than the tomb. It can be seen from the plan in Fig. 14 that the columbarium had been shut off from the adjoining tomb by a wall, measuring 1.35 m. thick, made of large stones cemented in place. Sometime after this wall was built, to seal off the columbarium from the tomb, an attempt was made to cut an arcosolium in the west wall of the tomb. When a break-through was made into the columbarium, the planned arcosolium was abandoned. Obviously the cutter who began the hewing of the arcosolium did not know of the existence of the columbarium to the west.

No artifacts were found within the columbarium; thus it is impossible to date its use, other than by the prevalence of this type of funerary provision in Palestine during the Roman period. One other columbarium was found in the area of the Bronze Age cemetery on the west slope of the mound (*Bronze Age Cemetery*, p. 64).

THE LAMPS

The 15 lamps from Loc. 138 (see Fig. 49 for photographs of 12 examples) were the principal artifacts found in the Roman tomb. Most of these lamps were discovered on the floor of the tomb proper, although one (P1075) came from an arcosolium at the back of the tomb chamber. Apparently these lamps had once belonged to the grave goods deposited in the loculi and arcosolia. When the burials were looted for the lead of the coffins (one piece, 12 by 9 cm., remained in the bottom of one loculus) the lamps were discarded by the robbers.

The collection of lamps is remarkably homogeneous. The top and the bottom were molded separately and then joined together so skilfully that the join can be detected generally only from the inside. The lower part has usually a low ring-base and in two instances it bears a potter's mark. P1100 (Fig. 49:1) has a "V" impressed within the ring of the base; and P1091 (Fig. 49:3) bears the impression of a cross with curved ends, which suggest the swastika motif. The tops of the lamps are decorated with volutes, circles, triangles, and herringbone patterns.

This type of lamp is well known from tombs at Jerusalem (Karm el-Sheikh, *QDAP*, Vol. 1, Pl. 6:11, 13:9, upper right; a tomb on the Nablus Road, *QDAP*, Vol. 4, Pl. 83:3, which is almost identical to our Fig. 51:4) and at Samaria (*Samaria* III, Fig. 88:10). Mrs. Crowfoot assigns the Samaria type to probably the 3rd-4th century A.D. (*Samaria* III, p. 373). Were it not for the complete absence of handles or "hinges" on our lamps they would fit satisfactorily into Charles A. Kennedy's Type 15, which he dates on the basis of a Silet edh-Dhahr parallel (O. R. Sellers and D. C. Baramki, in *Supplementary Studies*, 15-16, *BASOR*, fig. 38) to the 4th or early 5th century A.D. (*Berytus*, Vol. 14, Fasc. 2, p. 81).

THE DEFENSES OF THE CITY

During the five seasons of excavation at el-Jib we were able to trace in a number of places the lines of two city walls that had encircled the mound (Fig. 1). The earlier of the two defensive systems was encountered in Area 10, where its line runs outside but parallel to the later wall, and in Area 8/9, where it is inside the later line of defense. As the earlier city wall runs from northwest to southeast in Area 8 it merges with the later wall just before it reaches the tower (cf. *Water System*, Fig. 2). From that point onward around the eastern and southern part of the hill we found no sure trace of the earlier wall. It may be that the builders of the later defensive system utilized the foundation of the earlier wall, building on the same line as that followed by their predecessors; or it is possible that our exploratory trenches to the east (Area 17), to the south (Area 28), and to the west (Area 22, Trench I) did not cross the line of the earlier city wall.

The later city wall is more fully recorded. The following table gives the areas in which it was found, the length of each segment actually uncovered or traced, and its width in each area.

| | | Width | |
Area	Length of Segment	Maximum	Minimum
10/9	55.7 m.	3.0 m.	2.8 m.
8-A/B/C-10/11	13.4	4.0	
8-H/I/J-6/7/8	16.2	4.2	
8-L/M/N/O-1/2/3/4/5 (wall)	14.6	4.4	4.3
(tower)	12.0		
8/17	6.0	3.1	
17-R-13	8.7	3.5	
28-D/E-8	2.2	(3.3)	
22 (Trench I)	5.0	3.2	

From the contour map (Fig. 1) it can be seen that in the south the later city wall follows contour 770. As it circles the west of the hill it veers slightly inside this line until it reaches the northwest section of the tell, where it follows contour 773. It crosses the modern cemetery, which could not be excavated, and then runs in a fairly straight line to the southeast until it makes a sharp turn at contour 768. It is apparent from looking at the contour map that the builders of the later city wall planned it so as to make use of the maximum area of the mound for the enclosed city without sacrificing the precipitous scarp of the hill as a natural deterrent against attack by an enemy.

The circumference of the later city wall can be determined only approximately. In 1962 an attempt was made to measure with a 25-meter tape the exposed segments of the wall and what appeared to have been the course of the wall between the actual remnants. The first attempt yielded a measurement of 971 m.; on the second trial, when slightly different contours were followed, the total length was 959 m. A measurement of the line of the wall according to the scale of the contour map gave a figure of 932 m. The average figure of 954 m. may serve as a reasonable approximation of the circumference of the fortification.

The extent of the Early Bronze occupation of the tell cannot be determined exactly, since no trace of a city wall belonging to this period has been found. In 1956 there was discovered in Area 8 (Trench III, AB-1) a layer of approximately 1 m. of debris outside the outer (later) city wall. Imbedded in it were 14 Early Bronze Age storage jars, on which a roof had evidently collapsed (cf. *Water System*, p. 2). It is likely that this Early Bronze house stood within the city. This evidence, along with observations in a number of places that the builders of both the early and later city walls had cut through Early Bronze Age debris in digging foundation trenches, suggests that the occupation of the site in the Early Bronze period extended beyond the limits of the later cities.

That the later city wall had fallen into disuse by the early first century B.C. is apparent in Area 22 (Trench I), where a Roman pavement was found to have been built over it (p. 41).

The stones for the two massive fortifications for which we have remains were probably quarried from the edges of the hill on which the city was built as well as from the great pool-and-stairway (see *Water System*, p. 9, for the estimate of approximately 2,982 tons of stone taken from the cutting). When the tombs in Area 14/23 were cleared we found quarry marks in the soft layer of limestone which had attracted the tomb cutters in the Middle Bronze period (*Bronze Age Cemetery*, p. 41). While the actual evidence for the time of the cutting of building stone from the roofs of the Bronze Age tombs pointed only to the Byzantine period, it is probable that the area had been used as a quarry in earlier centuries.

The method used in quarrying is illustrated by three blocks only partly cut from the rock (Fig. 92), discovered in 1962 in the vicinity of Middle Bronze tombs found on the land of Mohammed Ali to the northwest of the tell. Three building stones had been partly separated from the living rock by deep trenches cut from the top. There remained only the final step in the removal, the breaking of the block free at the bottom. This could have been done by inserting wooden wedges in the grooves and wetting them with water to expand them sufficiently to shear the stone block loose from the bedrock. In this area, as well as in the area of the other Middle Bronze tombs, there are out-croppings of soft limestone suitable for cutting into building stones.

The precise dating of the city walls has been rendered difficult because of stone looting and erosion. With one exception (10-L-5, discussed below) we found no place where a floor level ran up to and joined the face of the city wall. In most places where segments of the city walls were encountered, only the foundation remained; the super-structure had been robbed completely by subsequent builders. This looting had destroyed the occupational debris which had accumulated in the houses beside the wall within the city. Most of the evidence which might have been used for dating the use of the city wall had succumbed to erosion.

The thoroughness with which the builders of the later city wall did their work complicates further the task of dating the remains. Those who built the later rampart trenched the accumulated debris to the bedrock in order to find a secure foundation for their wall. At one place (10-O-6) the trench was cut through 3 m. of earlier deposit. The debris from this foundation trench, 3 by 3 m., was then piled inside the line of the city wall and later levelled down to provide a floor for the houses inside the wall. When the city wall eventually fell into disuse and the stones were looted and used for other purposes at a later age, the winter rains washed the occupational debris contemporaneous with the use of the city wall down the steep sides of the natural hill, leaving only the filling of mixed sherds which had been packed beside the inner face of the fortification. Occasionally there remained good evidence for occupation at some distance within the city, but in no instance were there house walls or floors adjoining the inner face of the later city wall.

THE EARLIER WALL

Our best evidence for the earlier wall and its relation to the later defense system appears in 10-L-5. The chronological relationship of the outer to the inner city wall in this area can be seen in Fig. 21, even though the inner city wall had been almost completely robbed in this sector. Both the robber trench and the original foundation trench were discernible and are shown in the section. A yellow *huwwar* tip line (5) can be traced from the edge of the robber trench over the southeast wall of the house in 10-L-5 and over the stump of the outer city wall. Besides, another tip line (8) also continues over the foundation trench for the later (inner) city wall and continues in a northwest direction over the earlier house wall and the destroyed earlier (outer) city wall. It is clear that both the house and the outer city wall were either already out of use at the time of the construction of the larger inner city wall or were covered over at the time of its construction. Thus the inner city wall is obviously later than the outer one.

The house in 10-L-5 made use of the outer city wall as its northwest side (Fig. 89); the southwest wall had been completely robbed; at about the middle of the southeast wall there is a doorway through which there could be traced the floor of the last major occupation of the house before it was destroyed by the cutting of the foundation trench for the inner (later) city wall. The floor of this house was red in color (numbered 14 in Fig. 21). Over this floor there were found a small occupation level (numbered 13a in section), a white floor running to all walls (13), and an occupation level on top of the white floor (12). Those levels above the red floor (14) produced pottery which could have belonged to the Iron I Age, but the forms were so few and so indeterminate that no certain conclusions could be based upon it. From the detritus which separated the red floor (14) from the plaster floor (17) there were two sherds (Fig. 36:7 and 10) which indicate a date within the Iron I Age.

The collar-rim storage jar fragment (Fig. 36:10) belongs to the general type found in the Pre-fortress period (I) at Gibeah (*AASOR*, Vol. 34-35, Pl. 20:2, 4, 9, 13; Vol. 4, Pl. 28:24), dated to the 12th century B.C. (*BA*, Vol. 27, p. 53). The type is also known from Beth-Shemesh (*AS IV*, Pls. 40:1, 2, and 61: 1), Bethel (*BASOR*, No. 137, p. 7, Fig. 2), and other sites with remains of the Iron IA period (see *AASOR*, Vol. 34-35, pp. 16-18 for additional references given by L.A. Sinclair).

The plaster floor (17) was preserved only along the northwest side of the house (Fig. 21, and photo in Fig. 89). It was laid in two layers with a total thickness of ca. 8 cm. and was firmly joined to the outer city wall. Broken fragments of this plaster were found in various parts of Area 10, but only here was any portion of the floor in its original place. Immediately below this plaster floor there were found 5 rims in a hard, mixed level (Fig. 36: 9, 10-12, 14). The storage jar rim (Fig. 36: 12) has its closest parallels in the 12th century type found in the Pre-fortress period (I) at Gibeah, cited above. The cooking-pot rim (Fig. 36:9) is similar to a type found in the Fortress I and II at Gibeah, dated to the 11th century (*AASOR*, Vol. 34-35, Pl. 21:1, 10; Vol. 4, Pl. 25: 11). Since this type has been discussed recently by L. A. Sinclair (*AASOR*, Vol. 34-35, pp. 19-20) we have not given additional references to the type.

HOUSE WITH PILLARS

The house with pillars found in 10-M/N-4 is the most important structure discovered at the northwest of the tell. It is to be connected with the earlier of the two city walls, since the inner (later) city wall was built in a foundation trench that partly destroyed the house. The orientation of the main axis of the house is at right angles to the outer city wall; in addition, the absolute level of the plastered floor in 10-L-5 described above (770 m.) is approximately the same as that of the stone floor (Floor 3) of the house of pillars (769.83 m.). The outer walls of this building are not defined in every stage of its use, but the four stone pillars (Fig. 84) seem to have been utilized through two periods of its history.

According to the notes of William L. Reed, who supervised the excavation of 10-M-3/4, there were four levels observed in the area of the house. We shall list each as they were encountered in the course of the excavation.

a. Floor 1 was found about 80 cm. below the surface, to the east of Wall 2, which was a roughly built terrace wall dating to the Iron II period of occupation (Fig. 35:1-10). Unfortunately, houses associated with this floor did not appear in the area excavated.

b. Floor 2 was encountered at a depth of ca. 1.60 m. below the surface. This hard-packed floor of clay and bits of carbon covered the tops of the four columns in the building. Although there were no walls within the excavated area that could be associated with this floor, there was at the east side of 10-M-4 a ramp of packed clay which sloped upward in a rise of 0.5 m. over a horizontal distance of 3.85 m. toward the inner city wall (Fig. 83). The portion of the ramp which appears in the photograph is its surface which was cleaned in the balk between 10-M-4 and 10-N-4. A rough projection of the surface of the incline of the ramp in a line at right angles to the city wall would reach the line of the wall at about a meter or so above the preserved top of the foundation. It is obvious that the filling from which the ramp was constructed had come from the trench, 3 m. deep, which had been cut for the foundation of the inner city wall. The ramp had served as a means for getting the blocks of limestone of which the wall was built up to the level at which they were required in the process of building. A sample of the pottery from this level was saved and is shown in Fig. 35:11-25. It contains a mixture of Middle Bronze and Iron I forms. Surely it is the fill from the excavation of the trench for the later city wall. What was labeled Floor 2 at the time of excavation could have been only a temporary floor built upon the debris from the foundation trench. As the excavation proceeded in the plots to the northeast of 10-M-4 two other segments of a ramp were discovered. One of these appeared in the east balk of 10-N-5 (see Fig. 22 for drawing of the section and Fig. 86 for a photograph). There were two lines of limestone chips which indicate two successive ramps constructed for the building of the city wall. As the wall rose from the level where one ramp intersects the line of the city wall a new ramp was built. Another ramp was encountered in the east balk of 10-O-6 (Fig. 85).

c. Floor 3 consisted of a cobblestone pavement covered over with a beaten earth floor north of the line of the four columns, and a clay floor found in the small rooms (not shown on the plan) to the south of the columns. The four columns had been reused as a part of a poorly built wall (Fig. 84). Belonging to this period of short occupation were two ovens, each about 80 cm. in diameter (Fig. 82), at the southwest of 10-N-3. Pottery belonging to this period of occupation is shown in Fig. 36:1-6,8. Under Floor 3 at the northeast there appeared a burnt level which contained the pottery shown in Fig. 36:15-18. The two storage jar rims (Fig. 36:15, 16) correspond in type to the 12th and 11th century examples cited above, and the cooking pot (Fig. 36:18) has parallels in Gibeah Period II (11th century). Suggested parallels are listed in the Catalogue.

d. The primary use of the columns is represented by Floor 4, which consists of the pavement to the north of the columns (Fig. 84) and a pavement of flagstones found to the south of the row of columns. The latter is reported to have been broken in places where columns may have stood originally. Since no walls were found that can be dated to this period of use it is possible that stones were taken from them for the construction of walls in later periods.

The course of the outer (earlier) city wall was traced from the northwest corner of 10-J-3 through 10-N-6, a distance of 23 m. In this sector the width varies from 1.80 to 1.60 m. In an attempt to find the wall to the northeast of the segment mentioned above, a sounding was made in 10-O-8. Here the wall had been completely robbed and the robber trench filled with mixed debris. The city wall obviously crosses the cemetery at the north of the tell and was discovered again in 9-S-9, where it appears inside the later wall with a width of 2.60 m. This small segment seems to be a continuation of the inner city wall 8-I/J-5, where it measures 3 m. in width. At no place in the entire course of the inner wall on the northeast or east side of the hill do we have evidence of a floor coming directly against the face of the wall. Consequently it is difficult to date with certainty the use of the wall. It is certain from evidence in 8-G-6 (see below), where there is an Iron II house built across the line of the inner wall, that the inner wall on the east side of the hill is the older of the two. Since the two lines of fortification on the northwest side of the tell are roughly datable, it is tempting to assume that the outer wall there continues as the inner wall on the northeast side. The difficulty, however, lies in the measurements of 1.70 m. for the wall at the northwest and 2.60 m. for the continuation at the northeast. One possible explanation for this discrepancy in width is that the heavier defensive wall at the northeast was designed to afford a greater measure of security for the vital water system found in this area (*Water System*, pp. 1-2).

AREA 8-G-6

The levels of occupation found in 8-G-6 are of particular importance for establishing the relationship between the two city walls at the northeast part of the tell. From the plan in Fig. 18 it is apparent that the line of the inner city wall discovered in 9-T-9 and in 8-I-5 runs through 8-G-6. Below three levels of occupation there appeared three large stones (Fig. 23) which belonged to the foundation of the inner city wall. These stones from the remnant of the city wall had been used in the structure which was bounded by Walls A and D (Fig. 23). We shall describe each of the periods of occupation of this area as outlined in the notes of H. Neil Richardson, who supervised the excavation of this plot in 1959.

a. Period 1 is represented by an open court with a fireplace in its center. The courtyard was bounded by Wall A on the south, Wall D on the west, and the remnants of the earlier city wall at the east. The pottery from below the fireplace was reported to have been mixed, mainly sherds of Early Bronze with some Iron I sherds present. The end of this occupation is marked by a layer of ash which extended over the entire northern half of the plot; it did not extend south of Wall A, and hence does not show in the section (Fig. 24). A preponderance of Iron I pottery was reported from the burned level.

b. A plaster floor, 10 cm. thick, extended over the entire area north of Wall A and fragments of it were detected in other parts of the plot. The poorly preserved Wall E seems to have been associated with this plaster floor. The three pottery forms from the floor (Fig. 37: 1-3) belong to the horizon of the Iron II period. The ring-burnished bowl

(Fig. 37: 1) belongs to the period after about 840 B.C. if Miss Kenyon's date for the introduction of this type of burnishing is correct (*Samaria* III, p. 95).

c. The final phase of occupation here is represented by a beaten-earth floor extending over the entire plot. Walls B and C seem to be associated with it. During this period of occupation a small pit in the northeast corner of the plot cut through earlier levels. The pottery from this occupation is shown in Fig. 37:4-10. A 7th century date for the collection of bowls is most likely in view of the association of many of these forms with the royal stamped jar handles. The cooking pot (Fig. 37: 9) belongs to the Deep type and is similar to those at Tell Beit Mirsim which Albright assigned to Str. A_2 and dated to the occupation there after the end of the 7th century (*TBM* I, Par. 109).

LATER CITY WALL

The longest well-preserved stretch of the later city wall is in Area 10/9. Here the wall can be traced for a total distance of 55.7 m. from either foundations or robber trenches. The wall was built upon bedrock. The stones were hewn and roughly finished. From excavations in 10-O-6 it was apparent that a foundation ditch of the same width as the wall had been cut through approximately 3 m. of debris to the bedrock. The walls of the foundation trench had been used as a matrix for the building of the foundation for the wall. (Fig. 87). The foundation part of the wall had been laid in courses of larger stones filled in with smaller stones to level the courses. The careful fitting of the stones into layers of courses can be seen in 10-Q/R-8/9 (Fig. 90), where there is exposed a course of the stone structure at about the top of the foundation and the beginning of the wall proper.

The method for constructing the upper courses by means of ramps on which the stones were raised to the higher levels has been explained above (p. 36).

The fragment of wall appearing in 17-O/P-20 was built in a foundation trench cut through the deposit of Early Bronze Age debris. The house wall running northeast-southwest in 17-O-20 belongs to the Early Bronze Age and was cut by the trench in which the city wall was built. A gold ring with a design of two animals on the bezel (*Gibeon*, Fig. 77 and 78, where a Persian period date is suggested) was found in a crack within the top of the remaining city wall. Edith Porada has expressed the opinion that the piece shows reflections of the orientalizing style of Greece in the 7th century B.C. (*The Art Bulletin*, Vol. 45, p. 370). The end of the 7th century would thus be the *terminus ad quem* for the demolition of the city wall in this area, if the opinion of Miss Porada is correct.

In 17-R-13 there is a partly destroyed segment of a 3.50 m. city wall which is in an approximate line with the later city wall to the north. The construction, however, of this wall differs in that it is composed of two rows of large stones which serve as shells for a filling in the center (Fig. 88). It can be seen from the plan that in 17-S-13 there are remains of what may well be an earlier city wall outside the line of the better-preserved example. Since there was considerable disturbance in the area during the Roman period it was impossible to get any clear indication as to the date for the laying of the foundations of the city wall.

In Area 28 the city wall seems to follow contour line 770. A small segment of the city wall was found to be exposed toward the northeast, but a modern terrace wall prevented the exploration of its inside face. A trench in 28-D/E-8 disclosed a fragment of a city wall 3.30 m. wide, behind which was evidence for considerable Iron II occupation.

The final segment of the later city wall appears in Area 22, at the west of the trench (Trench I) cut in 1956. This excavation is described below (pp. 41-42).

DATES FOR THE CITY DEFENSES

The most extensive evidence for dating the construction of the earlier city wall appears in 10-L-5, where a portion of a well-laid plaster floor cemented to its face is preserved (Fig. 21). The evidence for a foundation trench for the earlier city wall a few centimeters below the plaster floor (Fig. 21, left) makes it likely that the plaster floor is roughly contemporary with the building of the city wall. The sherds found within the make-up for the plaster floor belong mostly to the 12th century, with a possible overlap into the 11th century. Since there is no evidence for any extensive occupation on the mound for the period of the Late Bronze Age, it is highly improbable that the earlier city wall was constructed before the 12th century. In the light of the available evidence, although it is admittedly scant, the building of the older city wall may reasonably be placed sometime within the 12th century (see *Water System*, p. 22, for a similar conclusion based on evidence which was available at the end of the 1957 season of excavation).

The date for the construction of the later city wall is difficult to fix precisely because, as has been noted above, there are no floors which run up to it. Several observations, however, may serve to place the date of its building within limits. First, its construction must have been later than the laying down of the occupational debris from which the large foundation trench in Area 10 was cut. A selection of pottery forms from the fill taken from the trench for the later city wall is shown in Fig. 35:11-25. As could be expected, the fill contained Middle Bronze and Iron I Age sherds, but there is no clear evidence for any forms which must be dated to a period later than the 11th century. Secondly, it has been seen that in 8-G-6 there was a layer of burning over the stub of the earlier city wall which contained sherds which belonged to the Iron I period. Thus it would seem that the earlier city wall had fallen into disuse before the end of the Iron I Age. Preserved from the layers of occupation above the burnt level in 8-G-6 are two samples of pottery, both of which are clearly within the horizon of the 9th-7th centuries. If the later city wall was built shortly after the destruction or abandonment of the earlier city wall, as it seems to have been, then it is reasonable to place its construction, until better evidence becomes available, within the 10th century.

How long the later city wall continued to be used is not clearly attested. Here again circumstantial evidence is of value. From the general picture of occupation of the site in the Iron II period it would seem that the city enjoyed one of its major periods of prosperity toward the end of the 7th century. There was an abundance of jar handles stamped with the royal stamp (*Hebrew Inscriptions*, pp. 18-26) and the Iron II pottery forms found within living areas correspond to those from the latest period of occupation at Tell Beit Mirsim A, a period which extends to the early part of the 6th century. Although there are pottery forms which may be dated as late as the end of the 6th century, these are limited in number and do not represent a major occupation at the site. Accordingly, there is reasonable ground for placing the destruction of the later city wall at about the end of the 7th century.

SOUNDINGS

A major handicap during the five seasons of work at el-Jib has been the lack of deep deposits of debris in any section of the mound. We have found evidence for settlements in the Early Bronze, Middle Bronze, Iron I, Iron II, and Roman periods, but in no place where we have been able to dig is there evidence for occupation throughout this entire span. It is therefore impossible to speak of general strata at this site. We have given below the results of three soundings where two or more strata were found; these representative samplings of the sequence of occupation at Gibeon supplement those which have already been given in the section on the city defenses and serve to provide a representative picture of the habitation of the mound during the major periods of the city's history. The variation in the picture of the periods of occupation found in the different parts of the mound may be explained by erosion and by the observation that in some periods the occupation of the entire top of the hill was not complete. It must be borne in mind that, as can be seem from the contour map (Fig. 1), the samplings of the occupation debris at el-Jib have been limited. Beside the practical consideration of cost, vineyards and orchards of olive and fig trees have been a deterrent to making soundings at the most advantageous places.

TRENCH I

The first sounding made at el-Jib when excavations were begun in 1956 was a trench, 5 m. wide by 35 m. long, cut on the west side of the tell in an area which was later designated as Area 22-B/F-15/16 (Fig. 1). Since the grid was not imposed upon the contour map until after work was completed in this sounding, we shall use the original designations of Trench I and plots E to M in the descriptions below. The plan for Trench I appears in Fig. 25, and the sections are shown in Fig. 26.

The most important results of this sounding are the following: (a) It has provided the best-preserved evidence for occupation of the site in the Roman period, although Roman pottery, coins, and fragments of house walls were found also at the east and at the south of the tell. Because of the fortunate discovery of a hoard of 23 coins of Alexander Jannaeus in the corner of a room of this area, the occupation there can be dated more closely by this hoard than would have been possible on the basis of pottery alone. (b) A well-preserved bath was discovered at the east end of the trench and can be associated with the Roman houses of the area. (c) A segment of the Iron II Age city wall was encountered running across the trench in plot G. We shall describe each of these features in turn.

ROMAN REMAINS

The only sure floor levels encountered in Trench I were those of houses of the Roman period, which appear clearly in the sections (Fig. 26) between Stratum 1 and Stratum 2. Several of the rooms could be clearly defined. The best preserved of these rooms is Loc. 1 in J-K, measuring 3 by 5.80 m., which has walls that measure about 70 cm. thick. The west wall of the room is not completely preserved but most probably had a doorway in it, connecting the room with Loc. 5 to the west.

Although the walls of the room which is marked Loc. 5 on the plan are not all stand-ing they probably formed a room which belonged to the same house as Loc. 1. The south wall of Loc. 1 probably continued westward to serve as the south wall of Loc. 5 as well. On the floor of Loc. 5 there were a juglet (Fig. 38: 15), a large storage jar *in situ* (Fig. 98), and other fragments of Roman pottery. At the northeast corner of the room there was discovered a cache of 23 coins of Alexander Jannaeus (103-76 B.C.). Although the dating of these coins is still a matter of debate (p. 52) it is reasonable to assign a date within the 1st century B.C. — probably the first half -- to the occupation of Loc. 5 and the adjoining Loc. 1, the floor of which is at approximately the same level.

Built hard against the east wall of Loc. 1 is the west wall of Loc. 6, which is roughly contemporaneous, although its floor was 17 cm. higher than that of Loc. 1. To the south of Loc. 6 was a fill, containing Roman and Iron II pottery, that was probably the debris from the construction of the bath to the southeast.

The bath (Fig. 25 for section and plan; Fig. 99 for photograph) is a small stepped pool, partly cut from the bedrock and partly built of stone above the rock. It is rectangu-lar in shape and measures 1.80 by 2.20 m. at the top. Its depth is 1.77 m., of which 1.30 m. is hewn from the bedrock. Both the surface of the rock cutting and the walls above are plastered with two layers of hard cement. The steps begin at the top on the south side and turn to the left to lead down to the small basin at the bottom. To the east of the northeast corner of the bath there is a well-built stone wall which is bonded to the side of the bath and which extends eastward. This is obviously a part of the struc-ture of which the bath was a part. To the south of this wall are traces of another masonry basin, 2.20 m. wide and 1.60 m. deep, which was also plastered (see Fig. 25 for plan). The entrance to both of these baths must have been to the south in the unexcavated portion.

The pottery found within the plastered bath near to the floor was consistently Roman in date (Fig. 38: 17, 18, 19). Sherds of a juglet identical with that found in Loc. 5 (Fig. 38: 15) and a fragment of a stone cup identical to the one from Stratum 1 of K-L (Fig. 38: 14) were found near the floor of the bath.

Another feature of the Roman occupation of the area is a circular bin, about 1 m. in diameter, in J immediately north of Loc. 5. To the west of this bin in H and G there are no clear structures of the Roman period. The great number of rocks in this area (see Fig. 25) suggests that there had been a pavement extending westward over the remains of the city wall of the Iron II period. When these stones were removed over an area of 50 sq. m. it was found that they rested on hard packed dirt in which there appeared nothing later than Iron II forms. It is thus apparent that in the Roman period of occupa-tion the city wall of the Iron II period was in disuse. The remains of the Roman settle-ment to the west of the city wall have probably been carried away in the process of erosion along the western rim of the tell.

Beyond the western edge of the city wall the excavation was extended for more than 10 m.; no building remains appeared, with the sole exception of a bottle-shaped cistern or vat cut into the bedrock just outside the edge of the wall (see plan of G in Fig. 25).

IRON II REMAINS

A segment of the city wall appears in plots G and H. What remains of it is probably foundation built solidly upon the bedrock. The wall runs approximately north and south and measures 3.20 m. in width. Four courses of stones are in place to a height of 1.90 m. The outer face is of larger stones and better built than is the inner face (see Fig. 26 for section of outer face and Fig. 97 for photograph). Parallel to this segment of the city wall is the only remaining contemporary wall running north and south between plots H and J. The wall is 60 cm. wide and its remains stand 1.25 m. above the bedrock on which it is built (Fig. 26 section). The pottery of the Iron II period shown in Fig. 38: 1-11 is from the fill below the floors of the Roman houses. It would seem that in the Iron II period the occupation level had been immediately above the bedrock and the hard packed clay found within the depressions in it, and that the fill of what is labeled Stratum 2 was washed down from higher levels at the east during the period between the abandonment of the Iron II city and the building of the houses of the Roman period.

SOUNDING IN 15-K/L-18

The sounding in 15-K/L-18 is unique among those made at el-Jib in that within the 4 meters of accumulated debris four distinct strata could be distinguished. Although the occupation had not been continuous — there is a gap between the Iron II and the Middle Bronze remains — the sounding did produce some clearly defined groups of artifacts which are definitely related stratigraphically. The notes on the stratigraphy are basically those of Diana Kirkbride, who supervised this sounding, rearranged for publication by Douglas M. Spence. The plans and sections for these two 5-meter plots are shown in Figs. 27-29.

From the surface to a depth of about one meter, the earlier remains had been disturbed by burials. All the graves were single burials in which the bodies had been interred with feet to the east, heads to the west, and faces looking south. Both adults and children were found. There was a larger number of burials in 15-L-18 than in 15-K-18, but in neither plot were any grave goods found. The pottery associated with the debris was reported to be Iron II with some Ommayad or late Byzantine examples.

NOTES ON 15-K-18

Level 1 lies immediately beneath the surface disturbed by the cemetery. It consists of two distinct phases and possibly a third. The uppermost phase is represented by Floor h (Fig. 28), which runs to Walls B and I (Fig. 27). This floor is of beaten earth and lime, and is found only to the east of Wall B. The lower phase of Level 1 consists of Floor i, which is of reddish earth and lime, and it also runs to Walls B and I. Between these two floors are traces of another earth and lime floor, but it is badly broken by the fall of a heavy wall.

Level 2 was separated from Level 1 by a stone fill (not apparent in south section, Fig. 28). This level consists of Floor j, which runs beneath Wall I and joins with Walls B and K (Fig. 27). A hole which may have been an inset for a storage jar was found cut into this floor. There are no traces of this level to the west of Wall B, and although later pits have disturbed the area, it seems apparent that Wall B was an outer house wall. To the west no residential remains were found. The pottery from this level was reported as Iron II.

Level 2 is founded on a deep artificial fill which was laid subsequent to the clearing off of earlier remains. Floor *k* represents the cleared surface on which this fill was laid. Beneath this fill the remains of Level 3 are quite well preserved in the east of 15-K-18, but are totally absent in the west. This level consists of three distinct phases. The upper phase is represented by Floor *l* (Fig. 28), which runs to Walls B and K (Fig. 27), and to the traces of Walls C and D which appear in the section of the balk (Fig. 28), but which were not recorded on the plan. This floor consists of well-laid, small, flat stones. In the southeast corner of the room formed by the four walls these stones abut the shoulder of a large storage jar which is set into the floor. To the north a circular basalt grinding stone with a hole cut through its center was found on this floor (Fig. 40: 12). The intermediate phase of this level is shown as Floor *m*, which is a pavement of large flat slabs very well laid in an irregular pattern, and which runs to the same walls as the floor of the phase above. This floor also adjoins the large storage jar, but whether it was built around the jar or was cut through at a later period could not be determined. The lower phase of Level 3 is represented by Floor *n*, which reaches to Walls B, C, D, and K. This floor is of *huwwar*. It was constructed on earlier remains, and represents the earliest phase of the Level 3 occupation. It has been cut to form a foundation trench for Wall C.

Stratum 4a lies immediately beneath Level 3. It was founded on Floor *o*, which runs only to Wall L. In contrast to the first three levels, Level 4a lies primarily in the western half of the plot. It is apparently the remains of a storage room which was destroyed by fire. The debris consisted of 30 cm. of burnt bricks, straw, and charcoal from roof beams. In the debris on the floor a large oblong grinding stone was found (Fig. 41: 20); on the floor itself were sixteen storage vessels, broken, but *in situ* (Fig. 91). Sunk into the floor at just over 1 m. from Wall L was a large stone, smooth on both faces and roughly squared at the edges. It rested on bedrock, and the floor of the room ran up and over its sides and then ended, forming immediately above the central part of the stone a circular depression which was filled with charcoal. This stone appears to have served as the foundation for a circular timber roof support (probably a tree trunk); the base had smouldered, but had not completely burned, during the general conflagration that destroyed the room. A sample of the charcoal from this depression was submitted to the Forest Products Laboratory of the United States Department of Agriculture in Madison, Wisconsin. It was identified as olive (letter from B. Francis Kukachka, Acting Chief, Division of Timber Growth and Utilization Relations, May 25, 1961).

Level 4b lies directly below the burnt floor of Level 4a and consists of two phases. The upper phase is represented by Floor *p*, which runs under Wall L in places and is cut by it elsewhere. It is therefore earlier than Wall L, but the walls to which it ran were not found. The lower phase of Level 4b consists of the occupational debris lying between bedrock and Floor *p*.

NOTES ON 15-L-18

The stratigraphy of 15-L-18 differs from that of 15-K-18 in that all three phases of Level 1 are clearly defined, Level 2 is much better preserved, Level 3 is represented only by traces, and Level 4 is less extensive.

The three phases of Level 1 are represented by Floors *a*, *b*, and *c* (Fig. 29). Floor *a* is of packed earth and lime and extends to Walls A, E, F, G, and H (Fig. 27). Floor *b* is another earth floor that runs beneath Wall A, but meets the remaining walls of Level 1. Floor c is of *huwwar* and is broken by heavy stone fall. It adjoins Walls E and G, but runs beneath Walls F and H, and joins an earlier phase of Wall F (not shown on plan).

Immediately beneath Floor c of Level 1 a small fill was encountered in which there were numerous stones. This fill was probably laid down by the occupants of Level 1 in preparation for buildings. Level 2 lies beneath this fill and evidences two occupation phases. The upper phase is represented by cobblestone Floor d, which is composed of small stones laid over and between a foundation of larger stones laid flat. Floor d runs to Walls G, E, and J. On the floor next to Wall J a small juglet was found unbroken (Fig. 44: 6). Wall J, though occupying approximately the same position as the two phases of Wall F in Level 1, is entirely separated from them.

Floor e represents the initial occupation phase of Level 2, is of packed earth, and has a small pit dug into it. Around and in this pit there are strong traces of burning. As with the cobbled floor above it, this floor joins Walls E and J, but it does not join Wall G. Instead, it runs beneath Wall G to a similar, but earlier wall against which G was built. This earlier wall is not shown on the plan.

No pottery from Floor e was saved, presumably because it was not distinctive. The pottery which does represent Level 2 is all from the cobbled Floor d, which is the most representative and important phase of this level. A deep artificial fill underlies Level 2 here, as it does in 15-K-18. Floor f represents the leveled-off surface on which the fill was laid.

Level 3 is represented only by small pockets of debris in the northeast section of the plot which are sealed by Floor f. This virtual absence of Level 3 remains is due, obviously, to the leveling operations of the builders of Level 2.

The remains of Level 4 lie directly beneath Floor f, except in the northeast sector, where they underlie the pockets of Level 3 debris. In contrast to 15-K-18 there is only one floor here which belongs to Level 4. This is Floor g which runs only to Walls M and N. A small juglet (Fig. 46: 8) was found in a pit that had been cut into this floor. In part of the plot a thick layer of debris is associated with this floor, but elsewhere this debris has been cut by later occupants. Beneath this floor there is a thin fill overlying the bedrock, which has been quarried in a series of steps about 70 cm. deep.

There is no direct structural relationship between Levels 1 and 2 in 15-K-18 and the corresponding levels in 15-L-18. Neither floors nor walls extend through the balk so as to be evident in both plots, since the balk contained a large wall that separated the two areas. This wall appears as Wall E in 15-L-18, and is possibly the same as Wall D in 15-K-18. On the basis of pottery, the equation of the levels in the two plots would seem to be justified. Similarly, there is no direct structural relationship between Levels 3 and 4 in 15-K-18 and the corresponding levels in 15-L-18. On the basis of the pottery, however, the equation of the levels seems justified.

THE POTTERY FROM LEVEL 1

The most characteristic feature of the ceramic remains from Level 1 is the very large number of bowls burnished inside and on the rim (Figs. 39: 5, 7-11, 14; 43: 1, 3, 4, 7, 8). In addition, there are two larger bowls or craters (Figs. 39: 17; 43: 6) burnished inside and on the rim, as well as two more bowls (Figs. 39: 4; 43: 2) burnished on the inside. This type of decoration was typical of Tell Beit Mirsim A_2 (*TBM* I, p. 79). Furthermore, there were no examples of burnishing on the outside of bowls. The horizon of the pottery of Level 1 seems to correspond to that of Beth-Shemesh IIc (see *APEF*, No. 2, Pls. 41, 44, 47 and Wright's remark that Tombs 5-6 are to be dated to the 7th century or early 6th in *AS IV*, p. 136). The most distinctive single artifact from Level 1 is the three-flanged, socketed arrowhead of bronze (Fig. 43: 22). This type of weapon has been found in Russian graves of the 7th century B.C. and associated with the great Scythian invasion of Syria in the late 7th century (see R.V. Nicholls, "Old Smyrna," *Annual of the British School at Athens*, Nos. 53-54, 1958-59, pp. 129-130; and *Lachish III*, pp. 385-86).

THE POTTERY FROM LEVEL 2

The scant evidence from Level 2 is not distinctive enough to be dated more closely than to the Iron II period. The body of a juglet in Fig. 44: 4 has parallels at Tell Beit Mirsim A (*TBM I*, Pl. 66: 14, 25, etc.). The lamp (Fig. 44: 7) is typologically earlier than the high-footed example from Level 1 (Fig. 39: 24). The other forms from Level 2 are not sufficiently distinctive to provide clues for fixing the stratum within narrow limits.

THE POTTERY FROM LEVEL 3

Although two of the bowls (Fig. 40: 1, 5) from Level 3 are burnished spirally on the inside and on the rim, as were examples from Level 1, there appears in this level a new type of burnishing. Fig. 40: 11 (also Fig. 40: 3, which may belong to the same vessel) exhibits hand-burnishing on the outside, a technique not found in the later Level 1. Furthermore, Fig. 40: 2 and 6 are burnished inside and on the rim but not in the more common spiral fashion. The appearance of both the spiral burnishing inside and the hand-burnishing inside and outside within the same level of debris suggests a date somewhere within the 9th century B.C. (see W.F. Albright, *TBM I*, p. 79, and K.M. Kenyon, *Samaria III*, p. 95). The storage jar rim shown in Fig. 45: 7 is similar in shape to a 9th century example found at Hazor in Stratum VIII in Area A (*Hazor II*, pl. 60: 6) and Fig. 45: 8 is analogous to other 9th century examples in Stratum VIII of Area A at Hazor (*Hazor II*, Pl. 60: 4, 7). The cooking pot in Fig. 40: 14 is a well-known type (see *Hazor II*, Pl. 69: 6, 9, 14, 17, etc. from Stratum VI of Area A, dated to the first half of the 8th century).

THE POTTERY FROM LEVEL 4

The platters are represented by two examples (Figs. 41: 3; 42: 10), both of which have inverted rims of the characteristic Middle Bronze II type. One flaring carinated bowl with marked shoulder and a ring base with recessed center (tomb classification D.4.a.) appeared in a fragment which was sufficient to make the identification certain (Fig. 42: 4). This and other fragments belonging to bowls were burnished (Figs. 42: 3, 11; 46: 4). A rim of a necked bowl appears in Fig. 42: 1. Parallels to these bowls appear in Tell Beit Mirsim E-D (*TBM Ia*, Pl. 10: 7, 9, platters from E). Albright states that shallow bowls of D are "virtually always with inverted rims" (*TBM I*, p. 23).

A fragment of the body and part of the handle of a burnished piriform juglet (Fig. 42: 9) and the handle and segment of the rim of a jar (Fig. 46: 5) can be identified among the sherds from Level 4. The twin handle and wide-mouth juglet shown in Fig. 46: 8 is almost entirely preserved.

Two types of cooking pots appear in Level 4: one is the heavy type with more or less vertical sides, with a rope moulding with finger indentations around the rim (Fig. 42: 2, 5); the other is a lighter ware, presumably with rounded bottom, and an outturned rim (Fig. 41: 8, 12, 19). Both of these types appear at Tell Beit Mirsim in D. The heavier ware is shown in *TBM* Ia, Pl. 13: 3-5; the lighter ware in *TBM* Ia, Pl. 13: 7, 9.

Storage jars are well documented in the pottery from Level 4. Most of the rims are flaring and elaborately profiled (Figs. 41: 4, 5, 6, 7, 9, 11, 16; 42: 12, 14, 15; 46: 6); only one has a plain flaring rim (Fig. 41: 10). The loop handles from the sides of jars are oval in section and thickened at the lower end (Figs. 41: 14, 18; 46: 1). Decoration in the form of horizontal lines, or combing, usually on the shoulder of the jar is common (Figs. 41: 4, 11; 42: 8, 13; 46: 2). Some examples of burnishing on storage jars appear (Figs. 41: 1, 13, 17; 42: 18) in the form of horizontal wheel-burnishing on the outside of the vessel. A herringbone design in the form of a rope-like band around the sharply angular shoulder of a large storage jar (Fig. 41: 13) appears on a sherd which may be a part of the same vessel to which the handle shown in Fig. 41: 17 belonged.

The storage jars represented from our Level 4 fit the type from Tell Beit Mirsim E-D. For the elaborately profiled rim see *TBM* Ia, Pls. 11: 3-7 (E); 14: 5, 10 (D). The combed decoration appears at Tell Beit Mirsim frequently in D (*TBM* I, Pls. 10: 10; 11: 18-21) and the rope band or herringbone motif is said by Albright to be ubiquitous on storage jars of D (*TBM* I, p. 20). The loop handle on the shoulder (Fig. 41: 17) has a parallel in D of Tell Beit Mirsim (*TBM* I, Pl. 41: 13).

With the exception of cooking pots, of which there are no examples from T15 at el-Jib, the pottery of Level 4 seems to correspond to forms found in T15. The profiled rims of the storage jars have their counterpart in Tomb 15 (*Bronze Age Cemetery*, Fig. 24: 90); platters with inverted rim (Figs. 41: 3; 42: 10) appear frequently in the tomb (*Bronze Age Cemetery*, Fig. 20: 6-14); and the carinated bowl in Fig. 42: 4 has a good parallel in Fig. 20: 28 of the tombs publication; the piriform juglet in Fig. 42: 9 is probably like the example from T15 shown in Fig. 22: 57 of the tombs; the jar with handle on shoulder in Fig. 41: 17 is matched by two examples, one from T18 (*Bronze Age Cemetery*, Fig. 26: 5, 6) and another from T11 (*Bronze Age Cemetery*, Fig. 16: 3). The almost complete juglet shown in Fig. 46: 8 is similar to one from Megiddo X (*Megiddo* II, Pl. 39: 4)

An examination of K. Kenyon's criteria for the classification of the Middle Bronze tomb material into five groups (*Jericho* I, pp. 268-270) suggests that our material from Level 4 fits best into Group III. The presence of storage jars excludes the possibility of Group I, while the piriform juglet rules out the placing of Level 4 material in Group V. The presence of the shoulder-handle jug in our material suggests the possibility of Group III, where this form first appears; and the carinated bowl (Fig. 42: 4) of the type D.4.a. would also point to Group III, where this type is present, although still rare. Certainly our material should be placed within Groups II-IV, and probably in Group III.

CONCLUSION

The pottery from Level 4 certainly falls within the period covered by Tell Beit Mirsim E-D, which Albright dates from the late 18th century through the period of Hyksos domination down until *ca.* 1560-1550 B.C. (*TBM* II, p. 60). Since Kenyon finds that the Jericho tomb material Group III mainly corresponds to TBM E, with an overlap into Group IV and that TBM D corresponds to Group V (*Jericho I*, p. 301), it would seem likely that our Level 4 does not quite reach the middle of the 16th century, when the Middle Bronze II period came to an end. On the basis of the present limited evidence I should be inclined to place Level 4 principally within the 17th century B.C.

IRON AGE HOUSES IN AREA 17

During the 1959 season an area southwest of the pool was excavated and proved to be an Iron Age residential section. On the grid this area is designated 17-F/I-18/20. In addition to a well-defined Iron II house, other building remains were found from the Iron I, Roman, and probably the Byzantine periods. Scattered pottery indicated an Early Bronze occupation.

The excavated area lies on the side of the tell, which slopes downward toward the northeast. From the fill, which included a large quantity of field stones and other extraneous debris, it was evident that the area had long been used as a dump. The initial sounding was made in 17-G-20. Immediately beneath the surface, the tops of two walls were found and further excavation revealed other non-related structures. A good quantity of Iron Age sherds was found, including an inscribed jar handle of the type found in the pool during the 1956 and 1957 excavations (cf. *BASOR*, No. 160, pp. 2 ff., inscription No. 61). It was then decided to enlarge the area of excavation, and the remaining plots were laid out.

The surface pottery was mixed, but the Iron Age forms were most frequent. Immediately beneath the surface the remains of several walls were encountered. It is impossible to date these walls with any accuracy as no definite floor levels were found in association with them. Certain observations, however, suggest that these surface remains belong to several occupational phases. One of these phases is represented by the north-south wall in 17-G-19/20, the north-south wall in 17-G/H-20, the east-west wall in 17-F-19/20, the fragment of an east-west wall in 17-G-19, and the adjoining north-south wall in 17-G-18 (Fig. 30). Occasionally two courses were found standing to a maximum height of 40 cm., but in most places only one course remained. These walls were found on hard-packed fill, and are apparently the foundations for the last structures which were built in the area. It is possible that these wall foundations are of Byzantine origin since the latest pottery evident in the area was reported as Byzantine, but this identification is by no means certain.

Another phase of construction is represented by the two north-south walls in 17-H-18 (Fig. 30). Although their top surface level and orientation are approximately the same as those of the walls in 17-F/H-19/20, other features make it unlikely that they are contemporary. In construction they are somewhat narrower, but even more distinguishing is the fact that their remains stand to a height of *ca*. 2 m. Between these walls the fill was of medium-sized stones without any soil to a depth of 1.9 m. Since the walls remain to such a height it would seem likely that this fill was placed there not long after their disuse in the building. The pottery associated with this fill was mixed: Byzantine, Roman, and Iron II. Beneath this fill was a 10 cm. layer of small rubble overlying a good floor on which was found pottery consistently reported as Iron II. Nonetheless, the walls themselves cannot be contemporary with other Iron II construction in this area. Their orientation, their height in relation to other walls known to be of Iron II date, and the fact that the wall to the west breaks through an Iron II wall make such dating quite unlikely. A date contemporary with the "Byzantine" walls is just as unlikely, because again the west wall, though paralleling and adjoining the north-south "Byzantine" wall in 17-H-19, extends to such a depth that it cannot be part of the same construction. It would seem more likely that the "Byzantine" walls are later, and that they were built around the upper part of the northern end of this earlier wall. The date of these walls would thus lie between the date of the Iron II and the "Byzantine" remains. Since the remains of a Roman structure lie directly to the east, it is possible that these walls are of Roman origin, although the buildings of which they were once a part do not remain.

The remaining structures which lie near the surface (Fig. 30) are also difficult to identify. The remains of the large bin shown in 17-H-20 first appeared ca. 50 cm. below the top of the remaining courses of the "Byzantine" walls. It is crudely constructed of medium-sized stones and extends to a depth of ca. 1.20 m. The pottery from above the bin walls was reported as a mixture of Byzantine and Iron Age forms, while the bin itself contained only Iron I and Iron II pottery. In addition, three bronze cosmetic spatulas (Fig. 51: 8, 9, 11), two stamp seals (Figs. 48: 25; 51: 14-16), a bronze bracelet-like object (Fig. 48: 23), and a piece of bronze plating (Fig. 51: 12) came from this bin. The bin was probably used as a dumping place for debris, and thus the contents can be of little help in dating its construction. Although unrelated to any other structures, the bin is possibly contemporary with the "Byzantine" walls.

In 17-F-20 are the remains of two walls which are oriented in such a manner as to be unrelated to the other walls (Fig. 30). No floor levels were found in relation to them. The northeast-southwest wall stood only one course high and was only partially preserved. The northwest-southeast wall was also poorly preserved in the northwest, but stood two courses high in the southeast. The pottery was reported as a mixture of Iron I and Iron II forms.

In 17-F-18/19 the remains of a bin appear (Fig. 30). The bin is constructed of large and medium-sized stones and its present remains stand to a height of ca. 60 cm. The larger stones are rectangular and stand on end. They were apparently reused from another structure. The pottery from this bin was a mixture of Iron I and Iron II, but the floor was reported to yield consistently Iron I forms. After the removal of the bin, Iron I sherds were found beneath the stones. It would seem that this general area is one of Iron Age debris into which the bin was cut at a later period. There were a number of large stones between the two phases of the north wall, but their relation to the bin is uncertain.

Further excavation revealed another series of structures (Fig. 31) beneath those described above (Fig. 30). For the most part they represent the remains of an Iron II house. In the west there appears what is probably an Iron I structure, while in the extreme southeast are the remains of a plastered basin belonging to the Roman period.

The Roman basin, in 17-I-18, was only partially excavated, since it was located next to a balk upon which rested a modern terrace wall. It is irregular in shape and is built against an earlier Iron II wall. The face of the north wall is plastered. No certain floor level was found. The pottery from the area above the structure was reported as a mixture of Byzantine and Iron II with a few Roman forms appearing. The debris from the basin itself, however, contained only Roman sherds. South of the basin no Roman forms appeared. Apart from this basin and its pottery the only definite evidence we have for Roman occupation in the area is a few pottery forms which appeared mostly near the surface in 17-G-18/20, 17-H-19, and 17-I-18/19 (though some were found at lower levels in a highly mixed fill). Three Roman coins also were found scattered through the remains. One (C62) was dated to Procurator Valerius Gratus (A.D. 15-26), another (C67), to a procurator under the emperor Augustus (name effaced), and the third (C64) may possibly be dated to Herod I (37-4 B.C.) (see pp. 53-62).

The most complete architectural remains in the area are from the Iron II period. They consist primarily of a four-room house surrounding a courtyard on three sides (Fig. 31 for plan; Figs. 93-96 for photographs). The floors of the rooms and courtyard are of packed earth and are all on approximately the same level. The walls rest on this floor; there are no foundation trenches. The courtyard (Loc. 123) is rectangular in shape, measuring 2.7 m. wide and 3.8 m. long, and is open to the north. A cylindrical stone surmounted by another of similar shape was found at the north end of the west wall of the courtyard. Corresponding to this feature is another cylindrical stone in the east wall of the court-yard and slightly to the north of the line of the courtyard. These two opposing features may have marked the entrance to the building. Doorways opened from the courtyard east-ward into Loc. W121, southward into Loc. 122, and westward into Loc. 124. On the floor of the courtyard were found about a dozen grape seeds, a stone roof-roller, an Iron II lamp, (Fig. 47: 4), five hand grindstones, and consistently Iron II sherds (Fig. 47: 15, 16).

The room adjoining the courtyard to the west is designated Loc. 124. It is a rec-tangular room 1.5 m. wide and 3.2 m. long. Its east, south, and west walls are fairly well preserved, though crudely constructed, and stand to a maximum height of 1.22 m. The re-mains of the north wall stand only two courses high. In the northwest corner of the room a bin was found, the floor of which was ca. 5 cm. lower than the room floor. On the floor of this room were found about fifty olive pits, several bone blades, a broken Iron II pitcher (Fig. 47: 11), an incised rectangular polishing flint, an Iron II lamp (Fig. 47: 5), two hand grindstones, and again consistently Iron II sherds. The doorway into this room is 70 cm. wide. Approximately 80 cm. above the floor, indentations which served ap-parently to secure the bolt of a door lock are cut into the stones on the north and south jambs.

The largest room of the complex is Loc. 122, which lies to the south of the court-yard. It is 5.5 m. long and has a maximum width of 2 m. The doorway from the courtyard into the room is 90 cm. wide. Since the western wall of this room, which stands 1.87 m. high, was over twice as thick as the other walls, it may have served as the support for a stairway which led to a second floor or to the roof. This possibility is strengthened somewhat by the observation that this is the only wall of the complex beneath which foundation stones were found. The south wall of Loc. 122 is poorly preserved in the west, and in the east it is missing completely. The removal of this eastern portion prob-ably resulted from the later construction of the two north-south walls which appear in 17-H-18 (Fig. 30). Clearly identifiable Iron II pottery (Fig. 47: 1, 3, 13, 14) and three hand grindstones were found on the floor. In the east wall is a 60 cm. doorway which leads into Loc. W118.

Loc. W118 is a small room 2.2 m. long and averages 1.55 m. in width. A circular bin, 1.15 m. in diameter and 1.20 m. deep, with slightly sloping sides, had been cut into the floor. This bin is plastered on the sides and bottom with a plaster of adobe type, some 3 cm. thick. The floor adjoining the top of the bin is of stone and lies on approximately the same level as the floor of Loc. 122. This floor then rises to form a slight step as it joins the wall on three sides. The pottery from this room and from the bin was consistently Iron II. The east wall is quite well preserved and stands to a maximum height of 1.7 m. The doorway on the west had been blocked up at a later period.

This blocking probably took place when the two later north-south walls in 17-H-18 (Fig. 30) were constructed. Loc. W118 was filled with large stones, as had been the space between the two high walls in 17-H-18. (On the plan a gap is shown in this south wall, but this is incorrect. This is the point where the later wall was built against and over its top surface, and this fact was not immediately recognized when the drawing was made.)

The final room of the house, Loc. W121, lies to the east of the courtyard. It is 1.3 m. wide, but its length is undefined as its north end extends into the balk. The east and west walls of this room require some comment. The west wall is constructed wholly of quite large hewn stones in contrast to the only occasional use of this type of stone in the other walls of the house. It would seem likely, therefore, that these hewn stones are from an earlier occupational phase and were reused by the builders of this Iron II house. The fact that this one wall is completely of large hewn stone seems to indicate that it was originally constructed at an earlier date and then reused as it stood by the Iron II occupants. The east wall of this room is also unusual in that it is two stones wide in contrast to the single-stone width of walls elsewhere in the house. Since only a short portion of this wall is exposed no reason can be given for this thickening. The pottery from this room, as elsewhere from the house, was reported as consistently Iron II.

Excavated in the area were three other loci which belong to the Iron II phase, but which are apparently not related to the house described above. Loc. 118 and 121 lie to the east of the house. Both have floors of hard-packed earth which are on the same level as the house floors. No doorways were found opening into either room. In the case of Loc. 121 it would seem likely that the entrance lies to the east where this room adjoins the balk. In Loc. 118 the doorway may have been to the west but later closed by the Roman construction which adjoins it on that side. The pottery from both loci was uniformly Iron II (Fig. 47: 2, 6, 8, 9, 10, 12).

Loc. SW122 lies to the south of the house and west of the area which had been disturbed by the construction of the two later north-south walls in 17-H-18 (Fig. 30). It appears to be a room, of which only the north and west walls remain. There are traces of a south wall, but the east wall was apparently completely destroyed when the later walls were built. At the north of this room is a *huwwar* floor, which lies *ca.* 50 cm. above the level of the house floors. The pottery from this floor was Iron II (Fig. 47: 7).

Although the Iron II walls were not removed, in four places (Loc. 122, 123, 124, and SW122) the floors were cut through to bedrock. In Loc. 123 and 124 the Iron II floors were found to be 5-8 cm. thick and of hard-packed dirt resting upon bedrock. In the west of Loc. 122 and in Loc. SW122 a 40 cm. level of debris from an earlier occupation was found beneath the Iron II floors. The sherds from this debris were reported as mostly Iron I, although some few Early Bronze and Middle Bronze forms also were reported. Beneath the northeast corner of Loc. SW122 the shallow remains of an unconnected wall were found which pass under the higher late wall. It lies beneath the Iron II level and is probably the remains of an Iron I wall which was not reused in the Iron II period (as was the west wall of Loc. W121).

Other evidence for the pre-Iron II occupation of this site is found in the western part of the area. In 17-F-18/20 and 17-G-20 a layer of debris was found which, on the basis of pottery, can reasonably be attributed to the Iron I period (Fig. 48: 14, 15, 21). Some of this pottery was found in association with the remains of floor levels and walls which, however, were so poorly preserved that a full picture is unobtainable. In parts of 17-F-18 a layer of debris *ca.* 20 cm. thick yielded pottery reported consistently as

Iron I, but not in association with any structures other than a small semicircle of stones surrounding a burned area which disappeared into the balk (not shown on the plan). In 17-F-19/20 the same layer of Iron I debris was encountered, and in addition the remains of what are probably Iron I walls. These walls are in a fragmentary state of preservation, but are founded at a depth which would relate them to the Iron I debris. Also, their construction is radically different from that of all the later walls encountered. They are built of large hewn stones ca. 60 cm. long and 45 cm. wide and consist of only a single row of stones. The large well-hewn stones which originally belonged to this wall were probably found to be useful in later constructions.

The evidence for Early Bronze and Middle Bronze occupation of the area is found only in 17-F-18/19. It consists of a thin layer of occupational debris immediately above bedrock, the pottery context of which was reported as being uniformly Early Bronze and Middle Bronze. No structures of any kind were associated with this debris as it covered only a small area in the west.

DATE FOR THE HOUSE

Since we have already described the various rooms of the Iron Age house (*Gibeon*, pp. 105-108), we need only discuss here the evidence for the last use of the building. The pottery shown in Fig. 47 (and rim of a stone vase in Fig. 47: 17) came from the rooms of the house (Fig. 31 for plan). The bowl in Fig. 47: 1 with spiral burnishing inside and on the rim suggests a date within the 8th and 7th centuries. The pitcher shown in Fig. 47: 11 is similar to types 584-588 at Tell en-Nasbeh (*TN* II, p. 17), which Wampler places between 700 and 500 B.C. (see also *Lachish* III, Pl. 86: 238, p. 292). Cooking pots (Fig. 47: 8, 9) are of the deep type and have a potter's mark incised on the handle; both probably had a second handle. However, Fig. 47: 14 is definitely a type with one handle (cf. *TN* II, Pl. 45: 955). The lamps with high foot (Fig. 47: 4, 5, and 7) belong toward the end of the Iron II period and the one example with slightly rounded base (Fig. 47: 6) is known to occur with the high-foot variety (*APEF*, Vol. 2, Pl. 47). The ring stand in Fig. 47: 2 is characteristic of the later part of the Iron II period at el-Jib and elsewhere. The only discordant piece of evidence for placing the house within the 8th-7th centuries is the pyxis in Fig. 47: 19. Since this jar is definitely a part of the Iron I tradition it must be considered intrusive.

The pottery and other objects found in unstratified debris in this section of Area 17 are shown in Figs. 48 and 51. Some of the objects, such as the seals, seal impressions, bronze tools and weapons, are of interest in themselves; others are shown as evidence for the general history of occupation at the site. In no cases do these objects throw light upon the dating of rooms or floor levels.

CATALOGUE OF COINS

During the five seasons 92 coins were found at el-Jib, of which 70 proved to be identifiable and are listed in the following catalogue. They were catalogued provisionally in the field by S. E. Johnson (1956), Asia G. Halaby (1959), and Gerald Cooke (1960). In the summer of 1961 Jane W. Sammis cleaned, recatalogued, and identified the coins with the aid of Edward Gans and George C. Miles of the American Numismatic Society in New York. Wolf Wirgin kindly looked at all the "Alexander Jannaeus" coins and classified them according to the types represented on plate VII of his (with S. Mandel) *The History of Coins and Symbols in Ancient Israel*, New York, 1958. His notations as to classification have been included in the catalogue.

All the coins are bronze except for those which are otherwise described in the catalogue. In the catalogue, the notation "Amman" at the end of the description indicates that the coin is to be found in the National Museum in Amman; all other coins belong to the University Museum, University of Pennsylvania, Philadelphia.

The 23 coins which were found in a hoard in 1956 are listed under the traditional attribution of Alexander Jannaeus, even though the identification of this well-known type has been seriously contested in recent years. Hill in *BMGC Pal.* listed this type as "imitations of Alexander Jannaeus," and characterized them as "wretched" coins which seem to have been issued by some successor to Alexander Jannaeus. Particularly relevant to the discussion of this type is A. Kindler's publication of the Jaffa hoard (*IEJ*, Vol. 4, pp. 170-185), in which she holds that this was but a provincial imitation of the Alexander Jannaeus prototype struck in Jerusalem (p. 184). One interesting difference between the Jaffa hoard and ours is in the distribution of the denominations. While the Jaffa hoard had only 5 coins of the large size, 220 of the medium, and 625 of the small, our hoard is about evenly divided between the large and the medium denominations; there are no examples of the small denomination. Wirgin (p. 88) is of the opinion that this type of coin is to be attributed to a period considerably later than the time of Alexander Jannaeus. In view of the fluid state of research on this problem we have adopted the more traditional view in the catalogue.

In the column where the provenience is listed, reference is sometimes made to the three trenches of the 1956 season. "I" designates the trench in Area 22-B/F-15/16; "II", the trench cut in Area 10-I/K-1 + 15-H/J-19/20; while "III" is used for the excavations around the pool-and-stairway in Area 8 (see plan in *Water System*, Fig. 2).

Serial No.	Field No.	Provenience	Diameter (mm.)	Weight (grams)	Description	Notes
					PTOLEMY II (284-247 B.C.)	
1	C39	III-E-1, surface	20	5.84	Head of Zeus, facing r. Reverse: eagle with club in l. field; inscription, ΠΤΟΛ[ΕΜΑ]ΙΟΥ [B]ΑΣΙΛΕωΣ. Mint of Tyre; no date.	Svoronos, Pl. XX: 19-20. Courtesy: ANS.
2	C78	17-P-11, .90 m. below surface	24	13.59	Head of Ptolemy, facing r. Reverse: eagle facing l.; date in field at r., ΛΓ, year 36 (250 B.C.) Silver.	Svoronos, cf. Pl. XXIII: 12. Courtesy: ANS.
					ANTIOCHUS III (223-187 B.C.)	
3	C53	8-G-5, surface	11	1.25	Laureate head of Apollo to r. Circle of dots. Reverse: Apollo stands on l., resting l. hand on bow and holding arrow in extended r. Probably mint of Antioch, c. 200 B.C.	E.T. Newell, The Coinage of the Western Seleucid Mints, Pl. XXVII: 14-15. Courtesy: ANS.
					SIDE IN PAMPHYLIA (3rd century B.C.)	
4	C55	17-M-9, .20 m. below surface	16	3.78	Helmeted head of Athena facing r. Reverse: pomegranate.	cf. G.F. Hill, Catalogue of the Greek Coins of Lycia, Pamphylia, and Pisidia, p. 150, Pl. XXVVIII: 4. Courtesy: ANS.
					EGYPTIAN OR PHOENICIAN (Hellenistic, probably 3rd century B.C.)	
5	C66	Sounding N-4, .30 m. below surface	7	0.10	Eagle stands front, looks l. Inscription to l. of three letters. Reverse: indistinct. Silver.	Courtesy: ANS.
					JOHN HYRCANUS I (135-104 B.C.)	
6	C57	8-F-7, .50 m. below surface	13	1.44	Inscription in laurel wreath: [yhw]hnn / [kh] hnhg / [dl]whbrh / [y]hdym. Reverse: double cornucopiae, between which poppyhead; border of dots.	BMGC Pal., p. 191, No. 23.
7	C54	8-H-6	12	1.24	Laurel wreath; inscription within effaced. Reverse: double cornucopiae, between which poppyhead; border of dots.	BMGC Pal., pp. 188-91 (?).

ALEXANDER JANNAEUS (103-76 B.C.)

Serial No.	Field No.	Provenience	Diameter (mm.)	Weight (grams)	Description	Notes
8	C7	I-J (hoard), Str. 1	12	0.98	Anchor in a circle; inscription around: illegible. Reverse: sun wheel in which rays are replaced by dots (?).	BMGC Pal., p. 209, Pl. XXII: 7 (?). Amman.
9	C8	I-J (hoard), Str. 1	10x13	0.73	Anchor in a circle; inscription around: illegible. Reverse: sun wheel of six rays; border of dots.	Wirgin, Pl. VII, obv. B, rev. C.
10	C13	I-J (hoard), Str. 1	9x12	0.55	Anchor in a circle; inscription around: illegible. Reverse: sun wheel; border of dots.	Wirgin, Pl. VII, obv. C, rev. C; Kindler, Pl. 16: 12, 14.
11	C14	I-J (hoard), Str. 1	11x12	0.99	Anchor in a circle; inscription around: illegible. Reverse: sun wheel; border of dots	Wirgin, Pl. VII, obv. B, rev. C.
12	C15	I-J (hoard), Str. 1	9	0.53	Anchor in a circle; inscription around, illegible. Reverse: sun wheel of six rays.	Wirgin, Pl. VII, obv. B, rev. C.
13	C16	I-J (hoard), Str. 1	14	1.10	Anchor in a circle; inscription around, [B]ΑCIΑ [EωC ΑΛΕΞΑΝΔΡΟΥ] Reverse: sun wheel; border of dots.	BMGC Pal., p. 209, Pl. XXII: 7. Amman.
14	C17	I-J (hoard), Str. 1	12x13	1.03	Anchor with one cross-bar in a circle; inscription around: illegible. Reverse: sun wheel with rays extending through border of dots.	Wirgin, Pl. VII, obv. C, rev. A; BMGC Pal., Pl. XXII: 11.
15	C18	I-J (hoard), Str. 1	10x12	0.53	Anchor in circle; inscription around, illegible. Reverse: obliterated.	Wirgin, Pl. VII, obv. B.
16	C19	I-J (hoard), Str. 1	11	0.91	Anchor in a circle. Reverse: sun wheel; poorly preserved.	Wirgin, Pl. VII, obv. B, rev. A; BMGC Pal., p. 211, Pl. XXII: 11.
17	C20	I-J (hoard), Str. 1	11x14	0.76	Anchor in a circle; thick dot in middle of stem. Reverse: obliterated.	Wirgin, Pl. VII, obv. G.
18	C21	I-J (hoard), Str. 1	10x14	0.86	Anchor in a circle; thick dot in middle of stem. Reverse: sun wheel; border of dots; inscription around, illegible.	Wirgin, Pl. VII, obv. G, rev. G.

Serial No.	Field No.	Provenience	Diameter (mm.)	Weight (grams)	Description	Notes
19	C22	I-J (hoard), Str. 1	11x13	1.11	Anchor in a circle; inscription, three letters unidentifiable. Reverse: sun wheel with rays extending through border of dots; inscription around, two letters resembling archaic Hebrew.	Wirgin, Pl. VII, obv. C, rev. G; *BMGC Pal.*, p. 211, Pl. XXII: 11; Kindler, Pl. 16: 18.
20	C23	I-J (hoard), Str. 1	8x13	0.61	Obliterated. Reverse: sun wheel.	Wirgin, Pl. VII, rev. G; Kindler, Pl. 16: 12, 14.
21	C24	I-J (hoard), Str. 1	9x12	0.51	Anchor in circle; thick dot in center of stem (?); inscription around, illegible. Reverse: sun wheel.	Wirgin, Pl. VII, obv. G, rev. G; Kindler, Pl. 16: 12, 14.
22	C25	I-J (hoard), Str. 1	8x12	0.64	Anchor in circle; inscription around, two letters resembling Greek. Reverse: obliterated.	Wirgin, Pl. VII, obv. G.
23	C26	I-J (hoard), Str. 1	10x11	0.62	Anchor in circle. Reverse: sun wheel; border of dots.	Wirgin, Pl. VII, obv. G, rev. G; Kindler, Pl. 16: 12, 14.
24	C27	I-J (hoard), Str. 1	8x12	0.53	Obliterated. Reverse: obliterated	
25	C28	I-J (hoard), Str. 1	10x12	0.95	Anchor in circle; inscription around, three letters. Reverse: sun wheel; border of dots.	Wirgin, Pl. VII, obv. B, rev. C.
26	C29	I-J (hoard), Str. 1	10x12	0.75	Anchor in circle; inscription around, three letters. Reverse: sun wheel; border of dots; inscription around, illegible.	Wirgin, Pl. VII, obv. B, rev. G; Kindler, Pl. 16: 12, 14.
27	C30	I-J (hoard), Str. 1	10x11	0.54	Blurred. Reverse: blurred.	
28	C31	I-J (hoard), Str. 1	10x11	0.59	Blurred. Reverse: blurred.	
29	C32	I-J (hoard), Str. 1	8x11	0.61	Probable anchor in circle; inscription around, illegible. Reverse: indistinct.	
30	C33	I-J (hoard), Str. 1	11x12	0.43	Anchor in circle; one cross-bar; inscription around: illegible. Reverse: sun wheel; border of dots.	Wirgin, Pl. VII, obv. B, rev. C.

Serial No.	Field No.	Provenience	Diameter (mm.)	Weight (grams)	Description	Notes
31	C36	1-H, .90 m. below surface	13	1.08	Anchor in circle; inscription around: illegible. Reverse: sun wheel of 8 rays with rays extending through border of dots.	BMGC Pal., p. 211, Pl. XXII: 11.
32	C69	Locus 201, 1.30 m. below surface	9.5	0.54	Anchor in circle; thick dot in middle of stem. Inscription around: illegible. Reverse: sun wheel; border of dots. Inscription around: illegible.	Wirgin, Pl. VII, obv. A, rev. C (?).
33	C84	17-P-11 (west room floor)	8x10	0.31	Anchor in circle. Reverse: fragment of sun wheel (?); circle of dots.	Wirgin, Pl. VII, obv. B, rev. G (?).

HEROD I (37-4 B.C.)

34	C9	III-C-2, surface	15	1.62	Anchor; around edge beginning on r. above, inscription: BACI HPω. Reverse: double cornucopiae with caduceus between horns.	BMGC Pal., p. 224, Pl. XXIV: 9 or 10. Amman.
35	C51	8-F-4, 1.15 m. below surface on east side	23	5.83	Tripod with lebes in field l.; border of dots; inscription around; BAΣIΛE[ωΣ H]PωΔOY Date: Lᴦ in field and P. Reverse: thymiaterion between two palm branches; border of dots.	BMGC Pal., p. 220, Pl. XXIII: 14-16; Reifenberg, Pl. 3: 26.
36	C64	17-G-20, 1 m. below surface	13x16	0.94	Anchor; inscription, obliterated. Reverse: war galley l. with oars (?); almost entirely obliterated.	Reifenberg, p. 43, No. 36; BMGC Pal., p. 227, Pl. XXIV: 18 (?).

TYRE (?) (c. 1st century B.C.)

37	C71	Locus 203, 1.20 m. below surface	18	5.40	Bust of Melkarth, facing r. Reverse: eagle facing l. Silver.	Courtesy: ANS.

PROCURATORS

(a) Under Augustus (A.D. 6-15)

38	C67	Locus 122, .80 m. below surface	16	1.53	Badly centered ear of barley; inscription around beginning below, KAICA[POC]. Reverse: palm tree with two branches of fruit; date across field, L (?).	BMGC Pal., p. 248, Pl. XXVII: 1.

Serial No.	Field No.	Provenience	Diameter (mm.)	Weight (grams)	Description	Notes
39	C62	17-1-18, .90 m. below surface	16	1.93	(b) Valerius Gratus (A.D. 15-26) Within a wreath, inscription, IOV ΛΙΑ Reverse: three formal lilies springing from a single base; across field; date, obliterated.	BMGC Pal., p. 253, Nos. 16 ff., Pl. XXVIII: 11, 12. Courtesy: ANS.
40	C75	Locus 208, .70 m. below surface	15	1.85	(c) Pontius Pilate (A.D. 29-30) Three ears of barley, the center upright, the others drooping, tied together by the stalks with two horizontal bands; around, beginning below on l., inscription, [IO]YAI[A KAICA]POC Reverse: vessel resembling a simpulum, with upright handle on r.; around, beginning below on l., inscription, [TIBIPEOYKAICA]POC[LIΓ]	BMGC Pal., p. 258, Pl. XXIX: 4.
41	C35	III-A-1, .60 m. below surface	17	2.32	ANTONIUS FELIX (A.D. 52-60) Within a wreath, tied at the bottom (the tie taking form X), inscription, I[O]Y [Λ]IAAΓ [P]IΠΠΙ [N]A Reverse: Two palm-branches crossed; between stalks, date, LIΔ (14 = A.D. 54); around, beginning above on r., inscription, [TIKΛΑΥΔΙΟ]CKAICAPΓ[ЄPM]	BMGC Pal., p. 261, Pl. XXIX: 11.

Serial No.	Field No.	Provenience	Diameter (mm.)	Weight (grams)	Description	Notes
42	C70	Locus 203, 1.65 m. below surface	16	2.13	Two oblong hexagonal shields with two spears crossed; around, beginning on r., inscription, ΑΡΝΕ[ΡωΚΛΑΥΚΑΙϹ] Reverse: palm tree with two bunches of fruit; above and below, inscription, [ΒΡΙΤ] and across field, date, [Λ]Α ΚΑΙ (14 = A.D. 54).	BMGC *Pal.*, p. 264, Pl. XXIX: 13, 14.
43	C42	III-E-3, .60 m. below surface	16	2.51	Palm branch; around, beginning below on l., inscription, ΛΕΚΑΙ[Ϲ]ΑΡ[ΟϹ] (5=A.D.58/9) Reverse: within an olive wreath, tied below (with X), inscription, ΝΕΡ ωΝΟ C	BMGC *Pal.*, p. 266, Pl. XXIX: 17.
44	C77	Locus 214, 1.65 m. below surface	16	2.19	Palm branch around; below, inscription, ΛΕΚ[ΑΙϹ]ΑΡΟϹ Reverse: olive wreath, tied below (with X); inscription, ΝΕΡ [ω]ΝΟ C	BMGC *Pal.*, p. 264, Pl. XXIX: 17.
					HEROD AGRIPPA I (A.D. 37-44)	
45	C1	III-A-1, surface	16	0.29	Umbrella with fringe; around, beginning above on r., inscription, [ΒΑϹΙΛΕωϹ ΑΓΡΙ]ΠΑ Reverse: three ears of barley issuing from between two leaves; across field, date, obliterated.	BMGC *Pal.*, p. 236, Pl. XXVI: 1. Amman.
46	C3	III-A-1, surface	17	2.0	Umbrella with fringe; around, beginning above on r., inscription, obliterated. Reverse: three ears of barley issuing from between two leaves; across field, date, obliterated.	BMGC *Pal.*, p. 236, Pl. XXVI: 2.

Serial No.	Field No.	Provenience	Diameter (mm.)	Weight (grams)	Description	Notes
47	C10	I-G	17	2.91	Umbrella with fringe; around, beginning above on r., inscription, [BACIΛA]Eω[CAΓPIΠA] Reverse: three ears of barley issuing from between two leaves; across field, date, LG (6 = A.D. 42/3).	BMGC Pal., p. 236, Pl. XXVI: 1.
48	C46	Tomb 3	18	2.89	Umbrella with fringe; around, beginning above on r., inscription, [BACIΛE]ωCAΓPIΠA Reverse: three ears of barley issuing from between two leaves; across field, date, [L]G (6 = A.D. 42/3).	BMGC Pal., p. 236, Pl. XXVI:1.
49	C72	Locus 203, 1.90 m. below surface, in floor 4	17	1.92	Umbrella with fringe; around, beginning above on r., inscription, BACI[ΛEωCAΓPIΠA] Reverse: three ears of barley issuing from between two leaves; across field, date, obliterated; border of dots.	BMGC Pal., p. 236, Pl. XXVI: 1.
50	C73	Locus 203, 1.20 m. below surface	16	1.76	Umbrella with fringe; around beginning above on r., inscription, [BACIΛE]ωCAΓPI[ΠA] Reverse: three ears of barley issuing from between two leaves; across field, date, obliterated, border of dots.	BMGC Pal., p. 236, Pl. XXVI: 1.
51	C76	17-O-7, .70 m. below surface	16	2.31	Umbrella with fringe; around, beginning above on r., inscription, BA[CIΛEωCAΓPIΠ]A Reverse: three ears of barley issuing from between two leaves; across field, date: [L]G (6 = A.D. 42/3).	BMGC Pal., p. 236, Pl. XXVI: 2.

Serial No.	Field No.	Provenience	Diameter (mm.)	Weight (grams)	Description	Notes
52	C79	17-P-11 1.60 m. below 1st beaten earth floor	16	2.12	Umbrella with fringe; around, beginning above on r., inscription, BACIΛЄωC[AΓPIΠΠA] Reverse: three ears of barley issuing from between two leaves; across field, date, LG (6 = A.D. 42/3); border of dots.	BMGC Pal., p. 236, Pl. XXVI: 1.
53	C81	17-P-11, 2.40 m. below surface, room 2	16	2.56	Umbrella with fringe; around, beginning above on r., inscription, BAC[IΛЄωCAΓPIΠΠA] border of dots. Reverse: three ears of barley issuing from between two leaves; across field, date: LG (6 = A.D. 42/3).	BMGC Pal., p. 236, Pl. XXVI: 2.
54	C86	17-P-11, 2.20 m. below surface	16	2.11	Umbrella with fringe; around, beginning above on r., inscription, BA[CIΛЄωC]A[ΓPIΠΠA]; border of dots. Reverse: three ears of barley issuing from between two leaves; across field, date, obliterated; border of dots.	BMGC Pal., p. 236, Pl. XXVI: 2.

DOMITIAN (A.D. 81-96)

Serial No.	Field No.	Provenience	Diameter (mm.)	Weight (grams)	Description	Notes
55	C68	17-P-11, 1.50 m. below surface	20x22	7.13	Laureate head of emperor facing l.; inscription around, indistinct. Reverse: wreath in center of which, SC. Mint: Antioch in Syria.	W. Wroth, *Catalogue of Greek Coins of Galatia, Cappadocia, and Syria,* London, 1899, p. 180-81, possibly No. 244. Courtesy: ANS.

GALLIENUS (A.D. 253-268)

Serial No.	Field No.	Provenience	Diameter (mm.)	Weight (grams)	Description	Notes
56	C88	17-R-13, 1 m. below surface	20	2.63	Obverse effaced. Reverse: Figure stands r., holds staff; inscription around, LUNA LUCIF. Below, date, PXV. Mint: Antioch.	RIC, Vol. V, Pt. 1, p. 185, No. 609; R. Gobl, NZ, Vol. 75, 1953, p. 29, No. 3 under 10. Emission.

Serial No.	Field No.	Provenience	Diameter (mm.)	Weight (grams)	Description	Notes
					CONSTANTINE I (A.D. 335-337)	
57	C87	17-Q-13, 1.70 m. below surface, east room, next to wall	16	2.09	Diadem and helmeted head of Roma facing l.; around, beginning on l., inscription, VRBS ROMA. Reverse: wolf facing l. and nourishing Romulus and Remus and looking at them; above them, two stars; between stars, two or three points; below, SMN[?].	Cohen, Vol. VII, p. 330, No. 17. P. Gerin, Die Münzen, Wien, 1921, p. 193, No. 1.
					CONSTANTINE II (A.D. 337-340) or CONSTANTIUS II (A.D. 323-361)	
58	C52	8-F-4, 1.15 m. below surface	16	1.06	Diadem, head of emperor facing r.; inscription, [C]ONSTAN[N]TI. Reverse: broken, badly damaged; figure, facing l. and piercing enemy (?), object to l. (?).	
					HERACLIUS (A.D. 610-641)	
59	C56	8-D-4, .40 m. below surface	25x27	10.11	Cross, to left, inscription, H[E]RACL. Reverse: large M, cross above, E below; beginning top left (reading down) inscription, ANNO; to r. date; l (partially effaced). Mint: Constantinople, 610/11. 40 nummi.	Wroth, I, p. 196 ff., Nos. 109-115. Courtesy: ANS.
					CONSTANS II (A.D. 641-651)	
60	C38	III-B-2, Str. 2	20x25	3.31	Emperor stands, holding long cross in r. hand, and globe cr. in l. Reverse: large M in center; above B and C; below line ш [(restruck?)	Wroth, I, p. 268 f, Nos. 101 ff. Courtesy: ANS.
					UMAYYAD	
61	C65	Balk 17-F-18/19, .60 m. below surface	18	4.93	Mint effaced, early 8th cent.	Courtesy: ANS.
62	C2	III-A-1, surface	16	2.38	Mint: Damascus, no date.	J. Walker, A Catalogue of the Arab-Byzantine and Post-reform Umaiyad Coins, Vol. 2, No. 819. Courtesy: ANS.

Serial No.	Field No.	Provenience	Diameter (mm.)	Weight (grams)	Description	Notes
63	C4	I-E, surface	23	5.12	ZANGID Nūr al-Dīn Maḥmūd, Damascus, 561 H./A.D. 1165-6.	Courtesy: ANS.
64	C44	III-D-0, surface	14	1.89	BAḤRI MAMLŪK Nasir al-Dīn Muḥammad, 693-4, 698-708, 709-741 H./A.D. 1293-1341. No mint, no date.	Courtesy: ANS.
65	C60	17-H-19, .90 m. below surface	15x17	1.94	MAMLŪK (15th century)	Courtesy: ANS.
66	C58	17-H-19, .10 m. below surface	15	0.67	LATE MAMLŪK (?) (Probably 15-16th century)	Courtesy: ANS.
67	C43	III-F-1, surface	15	1.37	BURJI MAMLŪK Qānsuh al-Ghūri, 906-922 H./ A.D. 1501-16. No mint, no date.	Courtesy: ANS.
68	C48	II-C-1, .40 m. below surface	18	2.92	OTTOMAN Suleyman I, 926-974 H./A.D. 1520-66. Damascus.	Courtesy: ANS.
69	C12	I-J, surface	16	8.87	MISR (Egypt, 17th century)	Courtesy: ANS.
70	C63	17-F-20, .45 m. below surface	20	4.45	MIṢR (Egypt, 19th century)	Courtesy: ANS.

APPENDIXES

APPENDIX A: REFERENCE CHART FOR CELLARS*

Locus Number	Area	Figures	Locus Number	Area	Figures
103	8-F-4	6	153	17-O-8	9
104	8-G-4	6, 60	154	17-N-8	
105	8-G-4	6, 57	155	17-N-6	10
106	8-F-5	6	200	17-N-10	8, 69
107	8-E-4	6	201	17-K/L-10	8
108	8-F-4	6	202	17-P-10	8
109	8-G-5	6	204	17-M-10	8, 64
112	8-D/E-4	6	208	17-O-10	11, 68
113	8-D-4	6	208s	17-O-10	11
114	8-E-4/5	6	209	17-O-10	11
115	8-E-5	6	209w	17-N-10	11
135	17-M-9	9	211	17-O-11	7, 11, 67, 68
136	17-N-9	9	212	17-O-11	7
137	17-N-9	9	213	17-O-12	7
138[1-6]	17-L/M-5/6	10	214	17-P-10	8
139	17-O-9	9	215	17-N-11	7
140	17-N-9	9	216	17-N-11	8, 65
141	17-N-8	9	217	17-O-6	10
142	17-M-8	9	218	17-O-6	10
143	17-L-7	10	219	17-N-12	7, 63
144	17-N-7	10	221	17-P-11	7
145	17-K-8	10	222	17-P-10	8
146	17-M-9	9	223	17-N-12	7
147	17-N-9	9	224	17-N-12	7
148	17-L-8	10	225	17-Q-11	11
149	17-O-8/9	9	226	17-Q-11	11
150	17-N-6	10	227	17-Q-11/12	11
151	17-N-6	10	228	17-P-10	8
152	17-O-9	9	229	17-O-5	10

* Area numbers having a first number 8 are in Area 8, see Fig. 2. Area numbers having a first number 17 are in Area 17, see Fig. 3. For plans of openings of cellars in Area 8, see Fig. 4. For plans of openings of cellars in Area 17 (except Loc. 154), see Fig. 5.

APPENDIX B. LOCATIONS OF CELLARS BY AREAS

Area Number	Locus Number
AREA 8	
8-D-4	113
8-E-4	107, 112
8-E-5	114, 115
8-F-4	103, 108
8-F-5	106
8-G-4	104, 105
8-G-5	109
AREA 17	
17-K-8	145
17-L-7	143
17-L-8	148
17-L-10	201
17-L/M-5/6	138[1,2,3,4,5,6]
17-M-8	142
17-M-9	135, 146
17-M-10	204
17-N-6	150, 151, 155
17-N-7	144
17-N-8	141, 154
17-N-9	136, 137, 140, 147
17-N-10	200, 209w
17-N-11	215, 216
17-N-12	219, 223, 224
17-O-5	229
17-O-6	217, 218
17-O-8	149, 153
17-O-9	139, 152
17-O-10	208, 208s, 209
17-O-11	211, 212
17-O-12	213
17-P-10	202, 214, 222, 228
17-P-11	221
17-Q-11	225, 226
17-Q-12	227

APPENDIX C: LIST OF UNPUBLISHED PLANS AND SECTIONS
ON FILE AT THE UNIVERSITY MUSEUM, PHILADELPHIA

1. Plan of 10-I/K-1+15-H/J-19-20, called Trench II in the 1956 season: fragmentary house walls.
2. Plan of 8-L-1+17-I/Q-18/20, 1959 season: fragments of house walls.
3. Plan of 28-D-8/14, 1962 season: house walls, cellars, and portion of city wall.
4. Section of cistern in 10-Q-3; sections of cellars in 28-D-8 and 28-D-9, 1962 season.
5. Sections of north and west balks of Trench I, M, 1956 season.
6. Section of north balk of Trench I, K-L, 1956 season.
7. Sections of east and west balks of Trench III, AB-1, and east balk of Trench III, AB-2, 1956 season.
8. Section of east balk of Loc. 203 in 17-P-9, 1959 season.
9. Section of north balk of 17-P-9, 1959 season.
10. Section of east balk of 17-O-6, 1959 season.

APPENDIX D: BIBLIOGRAPHY OF PRELIMINARY REPORTS

1956: *New York Times*, Sept. 9, 1956; *Illustrated London News*, Oct. 27, 1956, pp. 695-697; *Biblical Archaeologist*, Vol. 19, No. 4, Dec. 1956, pp. 66-75; *University Museum Bulletin*, Vol. 21, No. 1, March 1957, pp. 3-26.

1957: *New York Times*, Sept. 21, 1957; *Time*, Oct. 7, 1957, p. 74; *Saturday Evening Post*, Feb. 8, 1958, pp. 40-41, 87-90; *Illustrated London News*, March. 29, 1958, pp. 505-507; *University Museum Bulletin*, Vol. 22, No. 2, June 1958, pp. 13-24; *Christianity Today*, June 9, 1958, pp. 3-4.

1959: *New York Times*, Sept. 27, 1959; *Expedition*, Vol. 2, No. 1, Fall, 1959, pp. 17-25; *Supplement to Vetus Testamentum*, Vol. 7, Leiden, 1960, pp. 1-12; *Biblical Archaeologist*, Vol. 23, No. 1, Feb. 1960, pp. 23-29; *Illustrated London News*, Sept. 10, 1960, pp. 433-435.

1960: *The Times*, London, July 23, 1960; *Time*, Aug. 8, 1960, p. 69; *Illustrated London News*, Sept. 24, 1960, pp. 518-519; *Bulletin of the American Schools of Oriental Research*, No. 160, Dec. 1960, pp. 2-6; *Biblical Archaeologist*, Vol. 24, No. 1, Feb. 1961, pp. 19-24; *Expedition*, Vol. 3, No. 4, Summer, 1961, pp. 2-9.

1962: *Illustrated London News*, Sept. 22, 1962, pp. 440-443; *Expedition*, Vol. 5, No. 1, Fall, 1962, pp. 10-17; *Biblical Archaeologist*, Vol. 26, No. 1, Feb. 1963, pp. 27-30.

APPENDIX E: THE STAFF AT EL-JIB, 1956-1962

Terry Ball, draftsman, 1962
Grace Conklin, cataloguer, 1962
Gerald Cooke, cataloguer, 1960
Robert C. Dentan, supervisor, 1956
Asia G. Halaby, cataloguer, 1957, 1959; supervisor, 1960, 1962
T. Hartley Hall, IV, photographer and supervisor, 1956
Mohammed Hasan, supervisor, 1960
John Huesman, S.J., supervisor, 1959, 1962
Claus-Hunno Hunzinger, epigrapher, 1957
Jean H. Johnson, cataloguer, 1956
Sherman E. Johnson, administrative director, 1956
Diana Kirkbride, supervisor, 1960, 1962
Charles F. Kraft, cataloguer, 1962
Arnulf Kuschke, supervisor, 1960
Yusuf Labadi, supervisor, 1962
John L. McKenzie, S.J., supervisor, 1960
Hasan Mamluk, supervisor, 1959
Robert J. Marshall, supervisor, 1959
Gustav Materna, draftsman, 1959, 1960, 1962
Subhi Muhtadi, surveyor, 1956, 1957, 1959, 1960, 1962
Willard Oxtoby, supervisor, 1959
Marvin Pope, supervisor, 1959
James B. Pritchard, director, 1956, 1957, 1959, 1960, 1962
Mary B. Pritchard, supervisor, 1962
Sally Pritchard, supervisor, 1960
Anne Reed, cataloguer, 1962
William L. Reed, supervisor, 1959, 1962
H. Neil Richardson, supervisor, 1956, 1959
Marcia Rogers, architect, 1956
Willy Schottroff, supervisor, 1962
R.B.Y. Scott, cataloguer, 1959
Mohammed Shehadeh, draftsman, 1959
Kenneth Short, supervisor, 1960
Robert H. Smith, supervisor, 1959
Choan-seng Song, supervisor, 1959
Douglas M. Spence, supervisor, 1959, 1962
David Stewart, supervisor, 1962
Thorir Thordarson, supervisor, 1956
Fred V. Winnett, supervisor, 1957, 1959
Linda A. Witherill, draftsman, 1957

ILLUSTRATIONS AND CATALOGUE OF POTTERY

AND SMALL FINDS

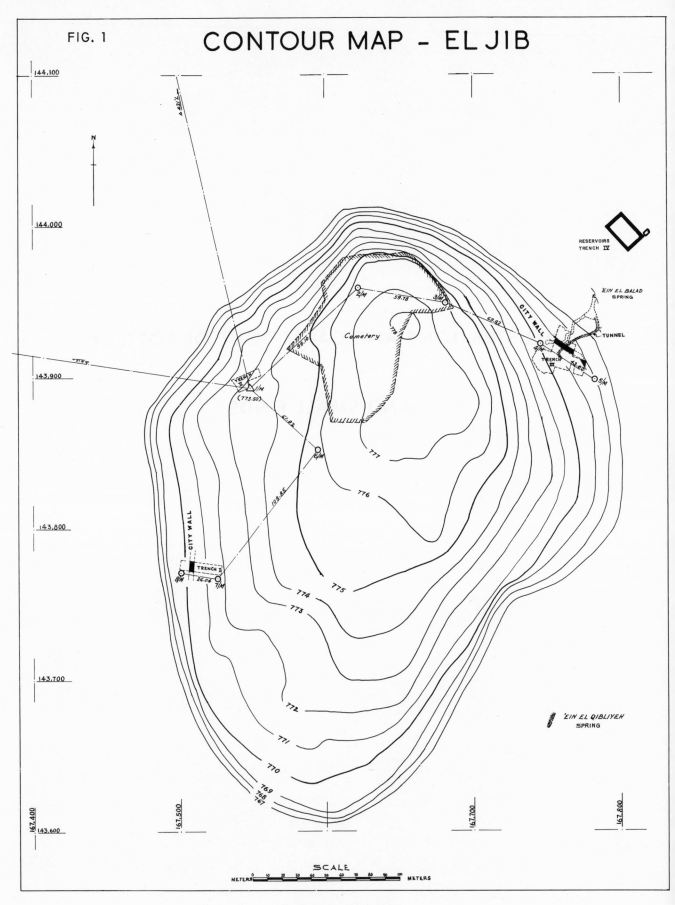

Contour Map of el-Jib

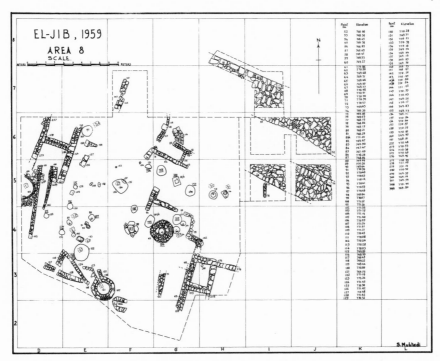

Fig. 2. General Plan of Winery in Area 8

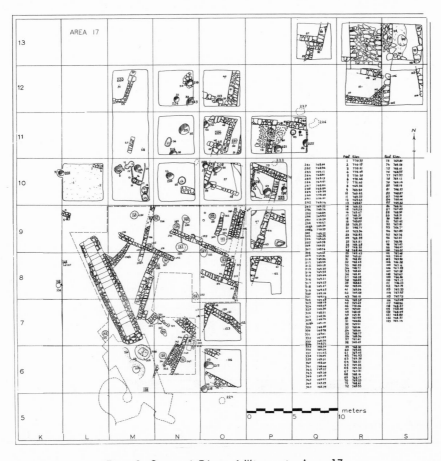

Fig. 3. General Plan of Winery in Area 17

FIG. 4

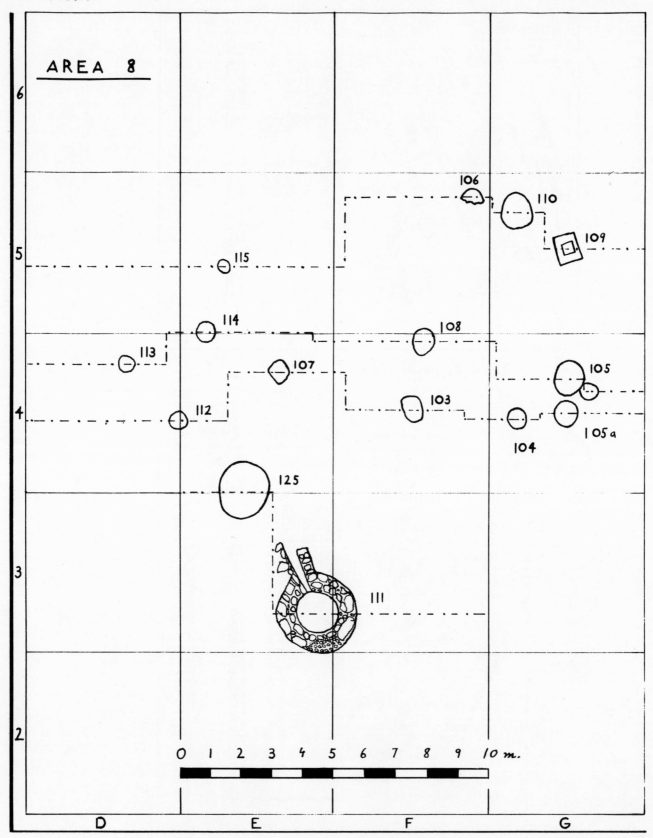

Plan of Opening to Cellars and Rock Cuttings in Area 8

FIG. 5

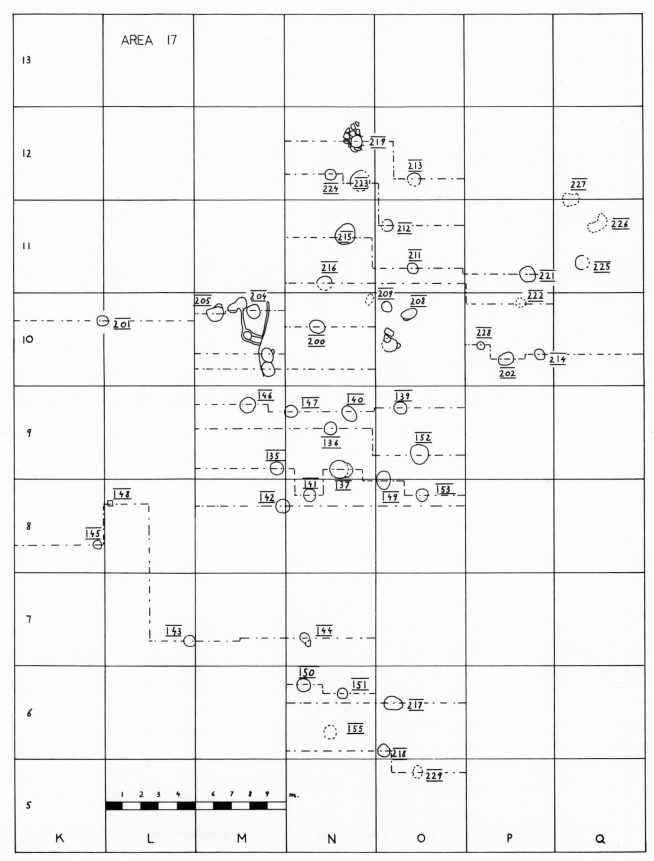

Plan of Openings to Cellars and Rock Cuttings in Area 17

FIG. 6

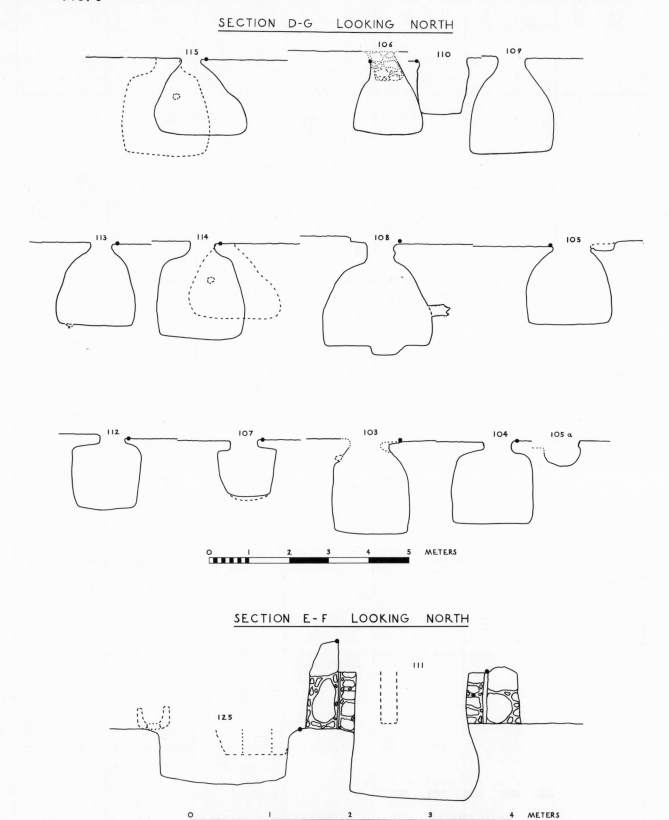

SECTION D-G LOOKING NORTH

SECTION E-F LOOKING NORTH

Sections of Cellars and Rock Cuttings in Area 8

FIG. 7

SECTION N - O   LOOKING NORTH

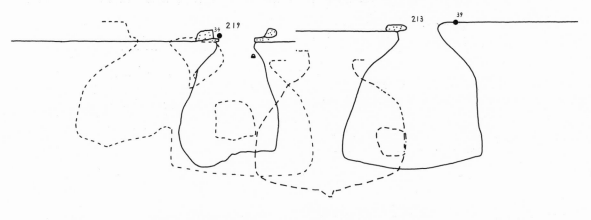

SECTION N - O   LOOKING NORTH

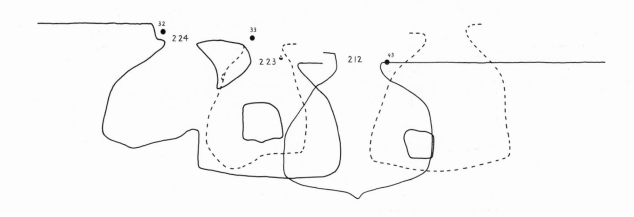

SECTION N - P   LOOKING NORTH

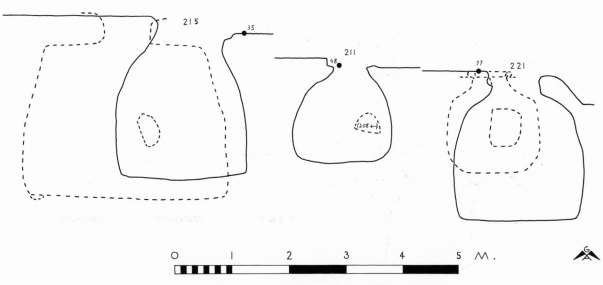

0   1   2   3   4   5 M.

Sections of Cellars in Area 17

FIG. 8

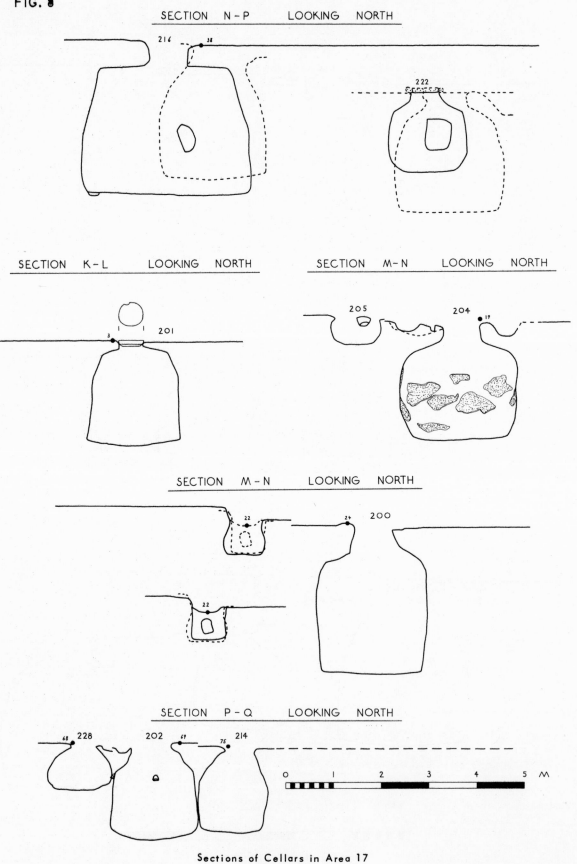

SECTION   N – P   LOOKING   NORTH

216   38

222

SECTION   K – L   LOOKING   NORTH

3   201

SECTION   M – N   LOOKING   NORTH

205

204   19

SECTION   M – N   LOOKING   NORTH

22

2+   200

22

SECTION   P – Q   LOOKING   NORTH

68   228   202   69   75   214

0   1   2   3   4   5 M

Sections of Cellars in Area 17

FIG. 9

SECTIONS M-O LOOKING NORTH

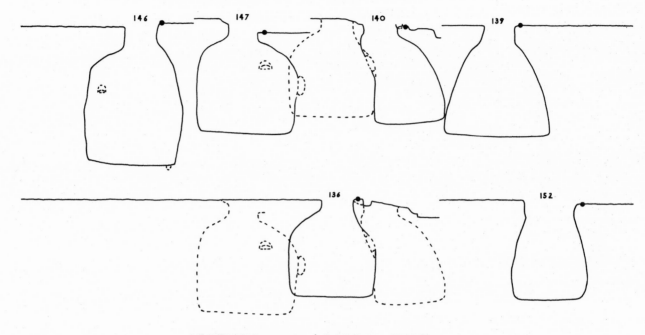

SECTIONS M-O LOOKING NORTH

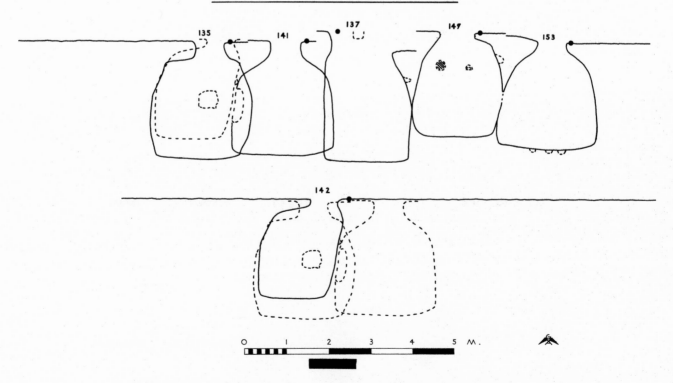

0   1   2   3   4   5 M.

Sections of Cellars in Area 17

FIG. 10

SECTIONS K-N LOOKING NORTH

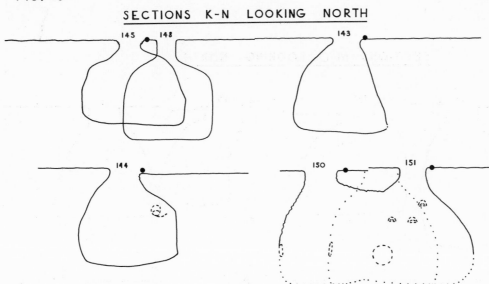

SECTION LOOKING EAST

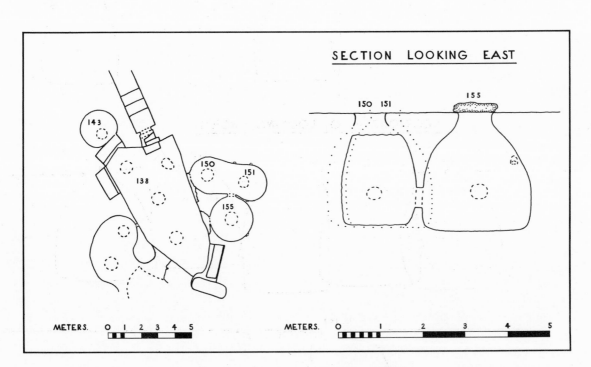

METERS. 0 1 2 3 4 5

METERS. 0   1   2   3   4   5

SECTION N-O LOOKING NORTH

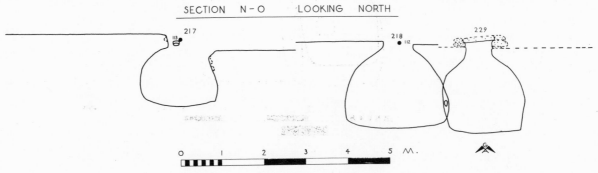

0   1   2   3   4   5 M.

Sections and Plans of Cellars in Area 17

FIG. 11

LOCUS 208-209

PLAN SECTION LOOKING NORTH

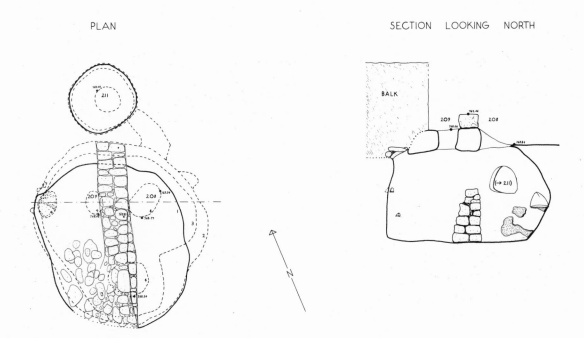

LOCUS 225-226-227

PLAN SECTION A-B

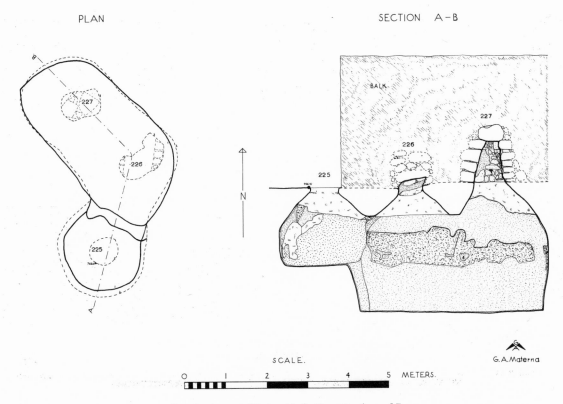

G. A. Materna

SCALE.

0   1   2   3   4   5   METERS.

Sections and Plans of Cellars in Area 17

FIG. 12

PLANS AND SECTIONS

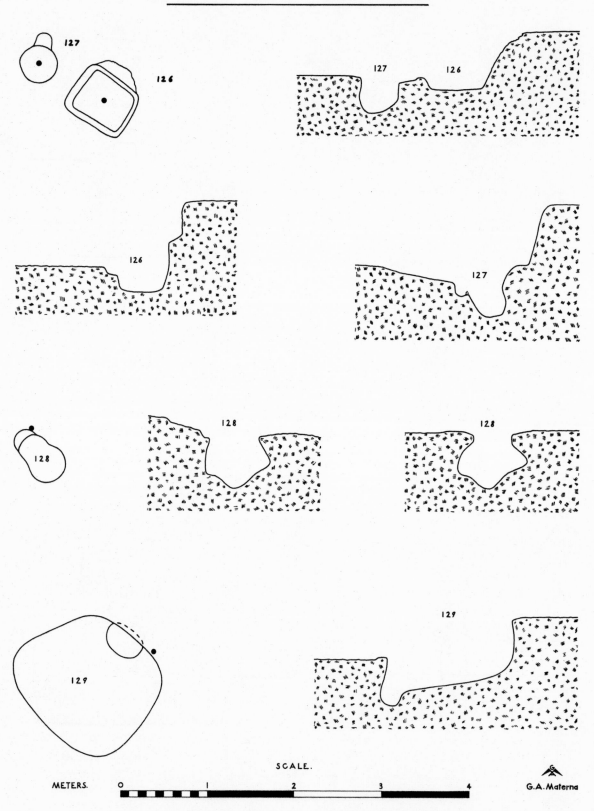

G.A. Materna

SCALE.

METERS. 0   1   2   3   4

Sections and Plans of Rock Cuttings in Area 8

FIG. 13

PLANS AND SECTIONS

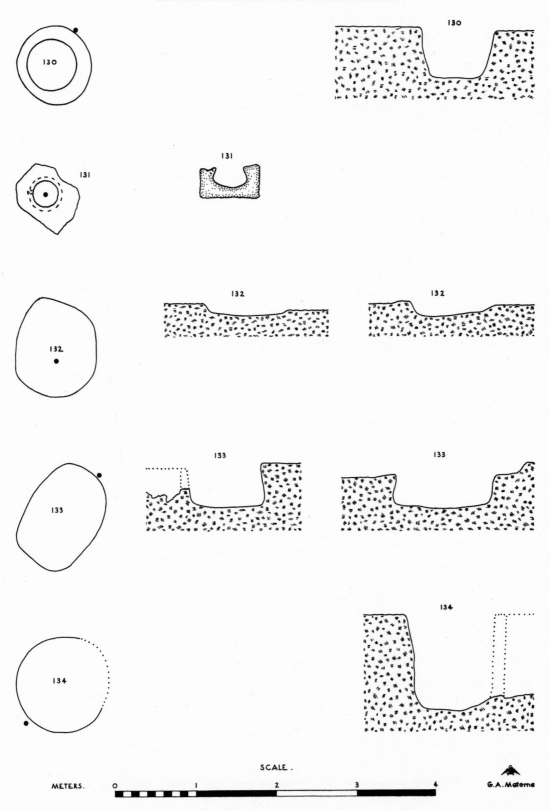

SCALE.

METERS. 0   1   2   3   4   G.A.Materns

Sections and Plans of Rock Cuttings in Area 8

FIG. 14

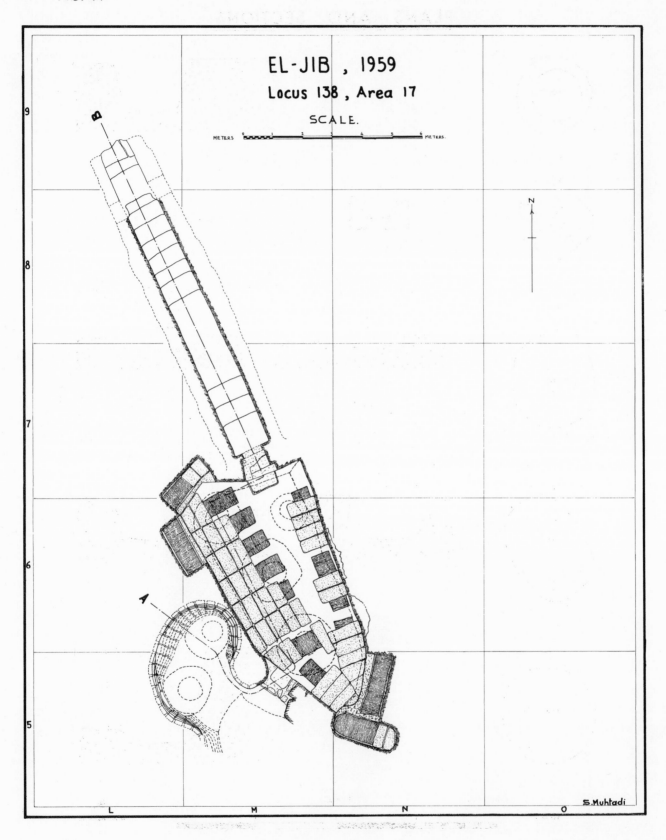

EL-JIB , 1959

Locus 138 , Area 17

SCALE.

S.Muhtadi

Plan of Tomb and Columbarium, Loc. 138

FIG. 15

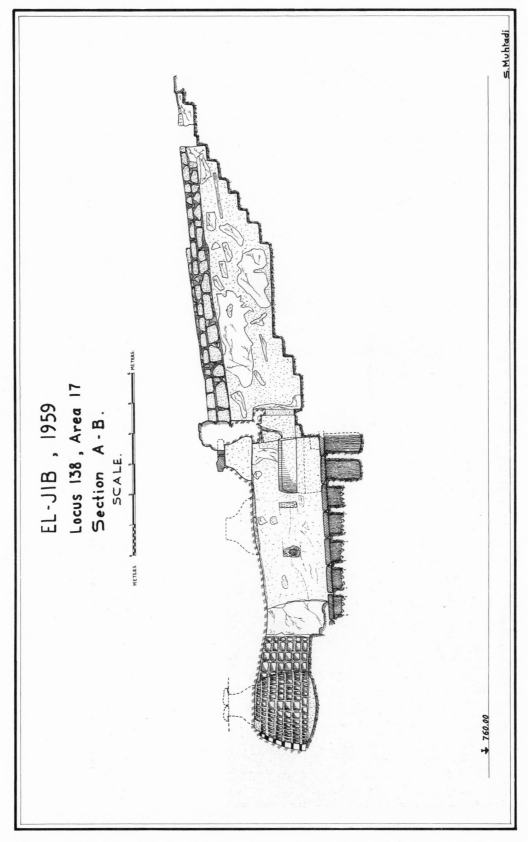

EL-JIB , 1959
Locus 138 , Area 17
Section A - B.

SCALE.

S. Muhtadi

↧ 760.00

Section of Tomb and Columbarium, Loc. 138

Drawing of Tomb and Columbarium, Loc. 138

Reconstruction of Frieze within Tomb, Loc. 138

FIG. 18

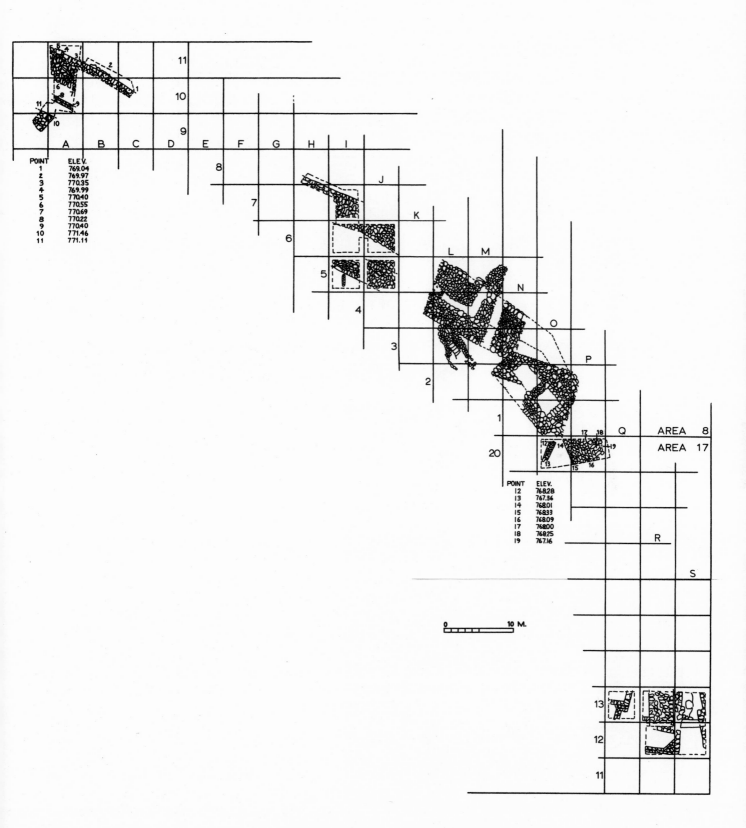

Plan of Defenses at Northeast of Tell

FIG. 19

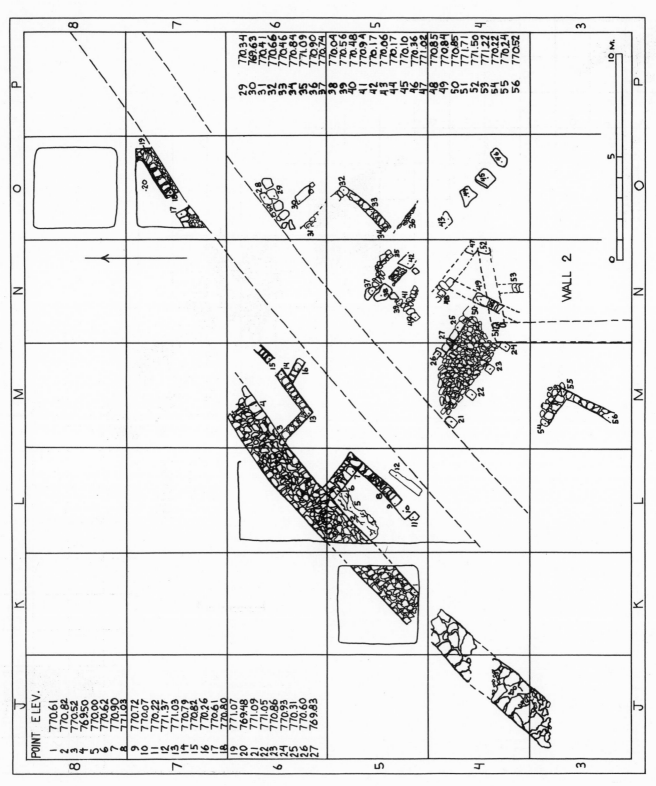

WALL 2

10 M.

Plan of Earlier Walls in Area 10

FIG. 20

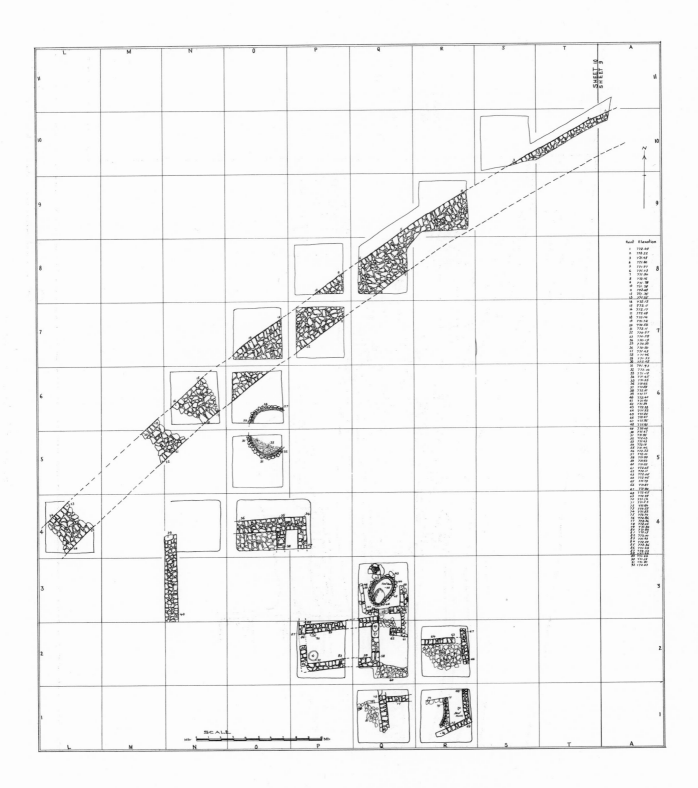

Plan of Later Walls in Area 10

FIG. 21

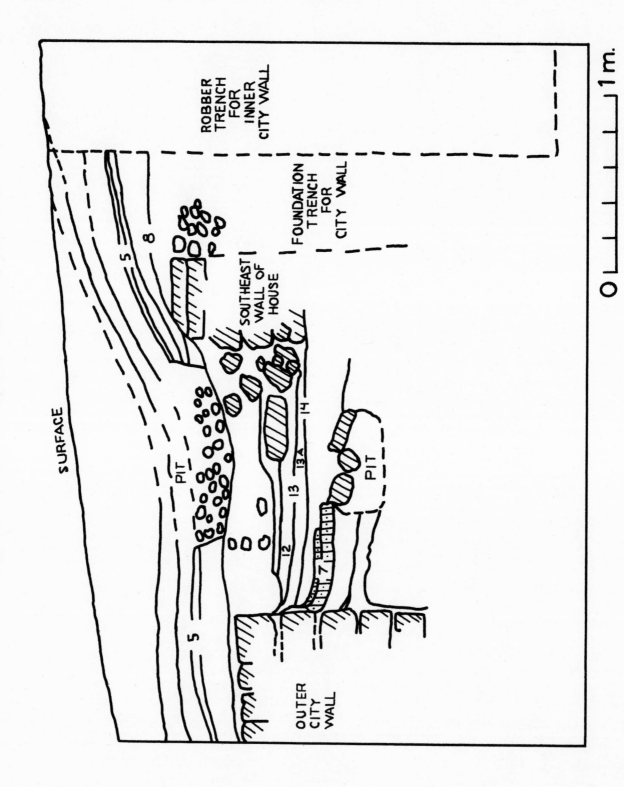

Section 10-L-5, Looking Northeast

Section of 10-L-5, Looking NE.

1 m.

SURFACE

ROBBER TRENCH FOR INNER CITY WALL

FOUNDATION TRENCH FOR CITY WALL

SOUTHEAST WALL OF HOUSE

PIT

5

8

14

13A

13

12

7

PIT

5

OUTER CITY WALL

FIG. 22

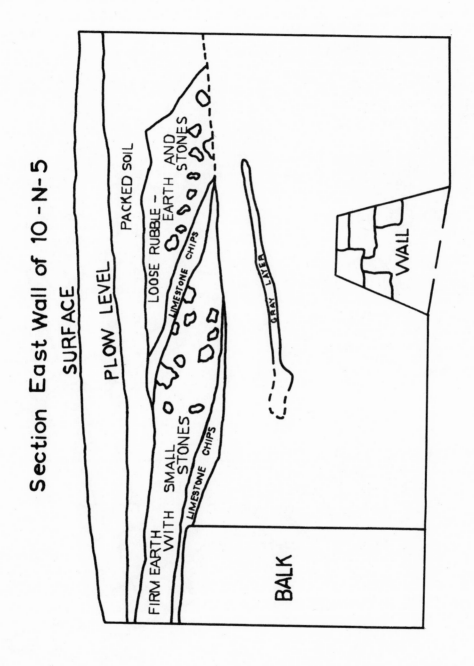

Section East Wall of 10-N-5

Section of 10-N-5, East Wall

1m.

FIG. 23

Plan of 8-G-6

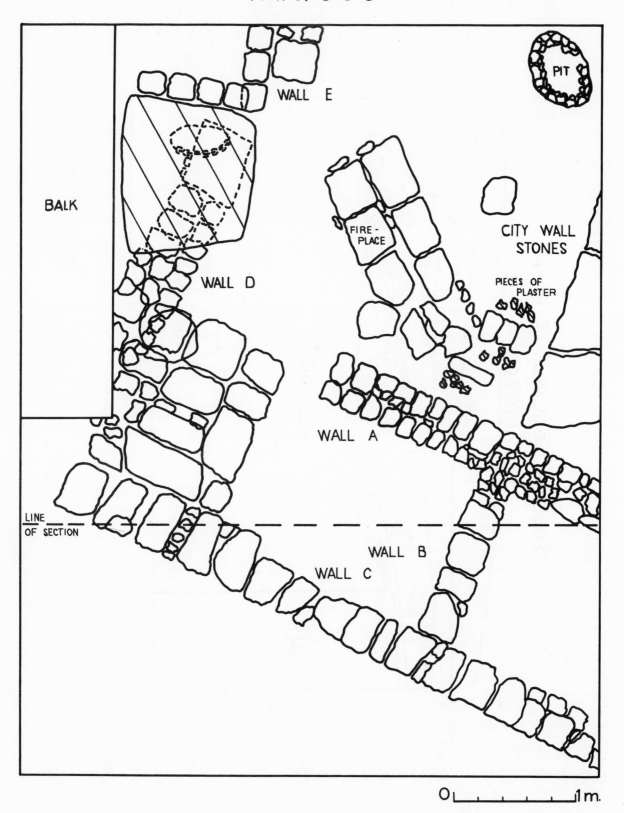

WALL E

PIT

BALK

FIRE-
PLACE

CITY WALL
STONES

WALL D

PIECES OF
PLASTER

WALL A

LINE
OF SECTION

WALL B

WALL C

0 ⌊_____⌋ 1 m.

Plan of 8-G-6

Section of South Balk, 8-G-6, Looking South

FIG. 24

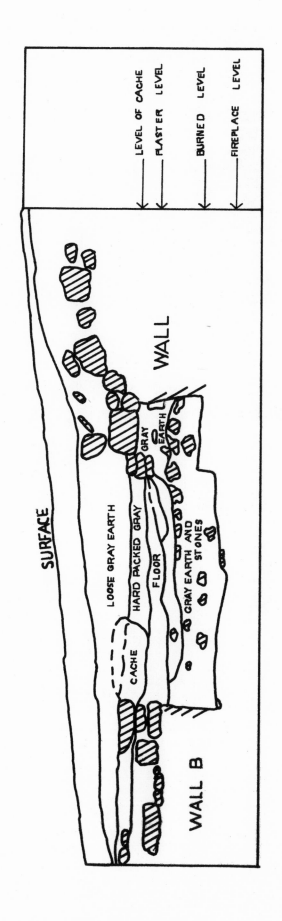

Section of 8-G-6, Looking S.

FIG. 25

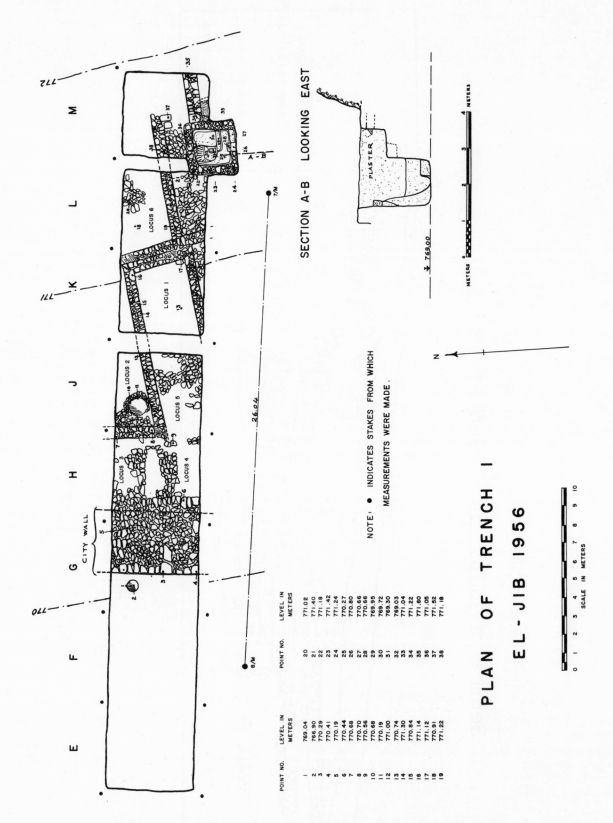

SECTION A-B LOOKING EAST

PLASTER

⊻ 769.00

METERS

SECTION A-B LOOKING EAST

NOTE: ● INDICATES STAKES FROM WHICH MEASUREMENTS WERE MADE.

POINT NO.	LEVEL IN METERS		POINT NO.	LEVEL IN METERS
1	769.04		20	771.02
2	766.90		21	771.40
3	770.29		22	771.18
4	770.41		23	771.42
5	770.19		24	771.24
6	770.44		25	770.27
7	770.68		26	770.80
8	770.70		27	770.66
9	770.56		28	770.66
10	770.68		29	769.95
11	770.19		30	769.72
12	771.00		31	769.30
13	770.74		32	769.03
14	771.30		33	771.04
15	770.84		34	771.22
16	771.14		35	771.60
17	771.12		36	771.05
18	770.91		37	771.52
19	771.22		38	771.18

PLAN OF TRENCH I

EL - JIB 1956

SCALE IN METERS

Plan of Trench I and Section of Bath

FIG. 26

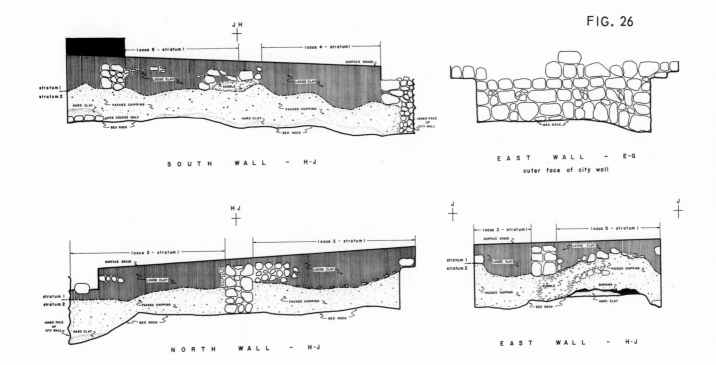

SOUTH WALL – H-J

EAST WALL – E-G
outer face of city wall

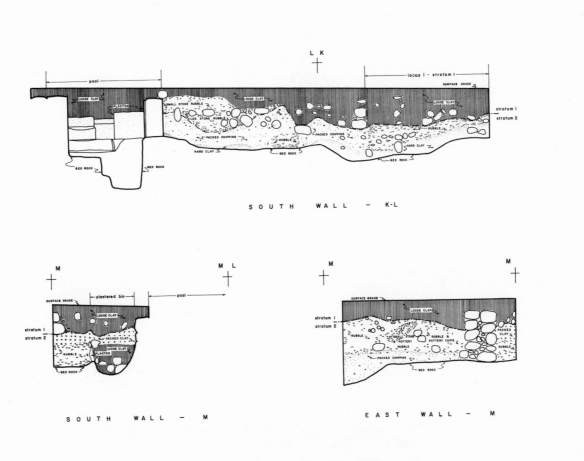

NORTH WALL – H-J

EAST WALL – H-J

SOUTH WALL – K-L

SOUTH WALL – M

EAST WALL – M

TRENCH I – EL-JIB 1956

Sections of Trench I

FIG. 27

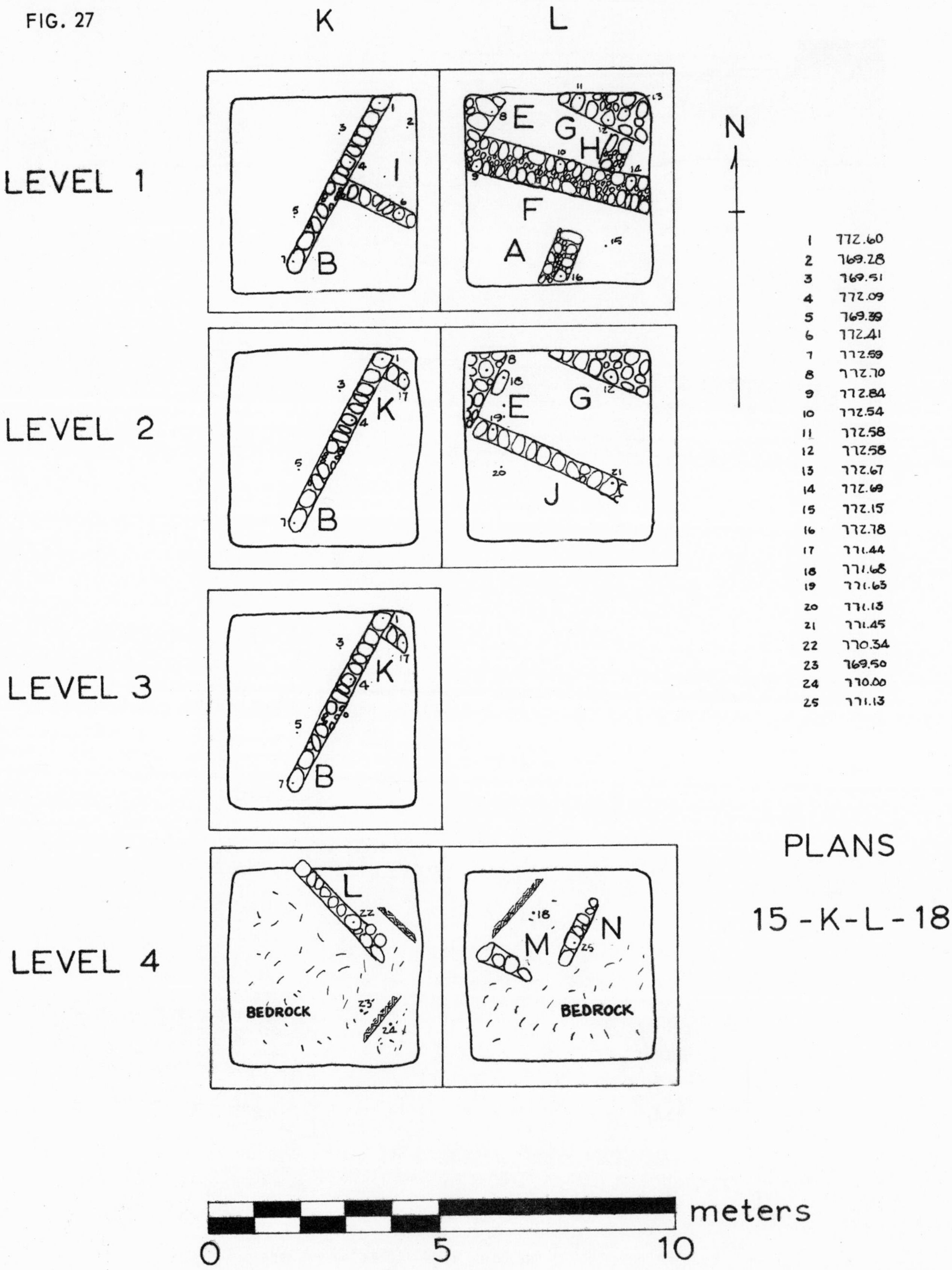

K   L

LEVEL 1

LEVEL 2

LEVEL 3

LEVEL 4

N

1	772.60
2	769.28
3	769.51
4	772.09
5	769.39
6	772.41
7	772.59
8	772.70
9	772.84
10	772.54
11	772.58
12	772.58
13	772.67
14	772.69
15	772.15
16	772.78
17	771.44
18	771.68
19	771.63
20	771.13
21	771.45
22	770.34
23	769.50
24	770.00
25	771.13

PLANS

15 - K - L - 18

meters

0   5   10

Plan of 15-K/L-18

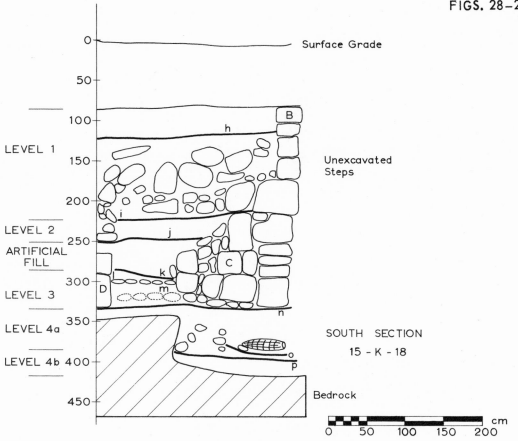

Fig.28. Section of 15-K-18

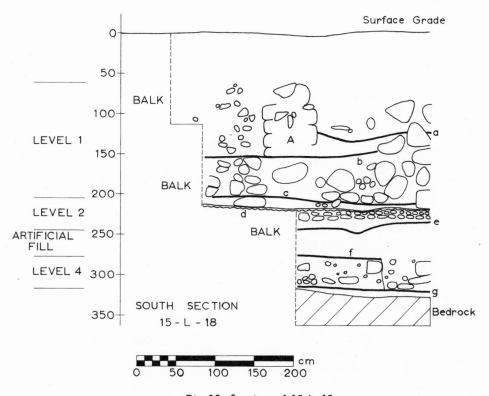

Fig.29. Section of 15-L-18

FIG. 30

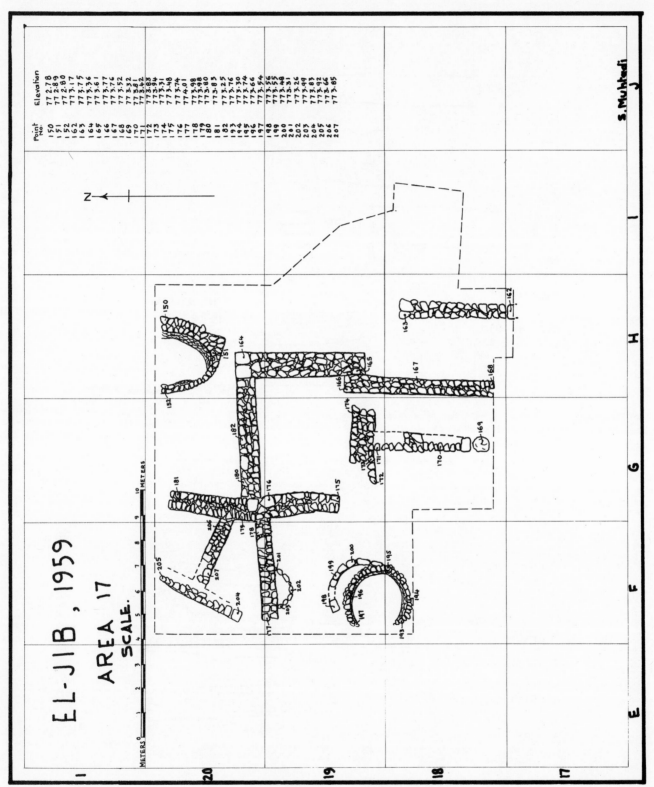

Houses of Area 17, Later Plan

FIG. 31

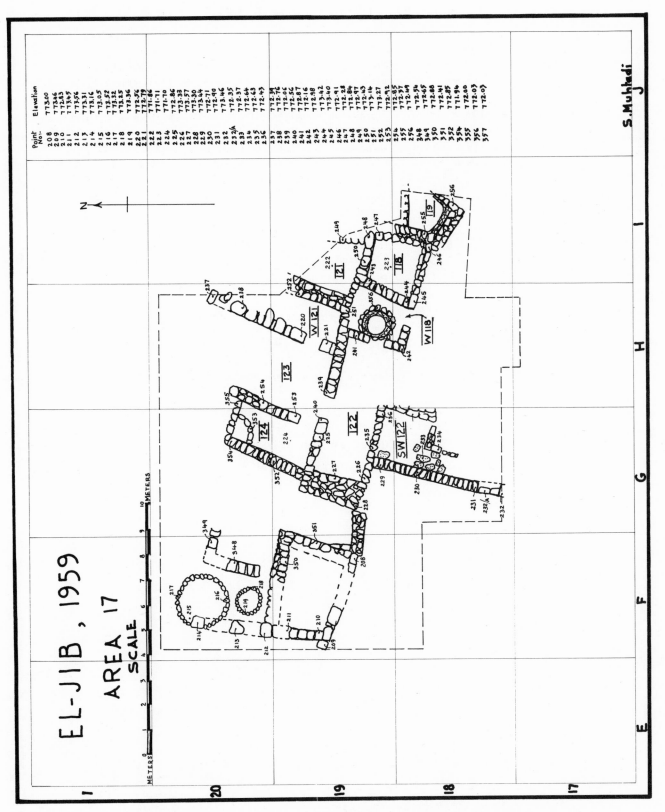

Houses of Area 17, Earlier Plan

FIGURE 32: POTTERY FROM WINERY

No.	Field No.	Provenience	
1	P901	Loc. 104, 1.55 m. above floor	Pitcher; reddish-brown ware, with many small white grits; cf. *Beth-zur*, Pl. 11:1, 2, *BASOR*, No. 151, pp. 16-27, Fig. 2:5-8.
2	P1069	Loc. 135	Storage jar; pinkish-buff ware, with small white and some red grits; see Fig. 32:8-11.
3	P948	Loc. 112, .60 m. above floor	Hole-mouth jar; reddish-brown ware, with few white grits, see Figs. 32:5, 33:11; *Lachish* III, Pl. 96:503, and p. 317 for other references.
4	P1087	Loc. 141, .70 m. above floor	Storage jar; light brown ware; *Lachish* III, Pl. 94: 481; *Samaria* III, Fig. 12a:1 (Period VIII).
5	P953	Loc. 112, .15 m. above floor	Hole-mouth jar; reddish-brown ware, with few white grits, four handles; see Fig. 32:3; *Lachish* III, Pl. 96:502, p. 317; *Samaria* III, Fig. 32:2 (Period VII-VIII).
6	P1083	Loc. 141, .90-1.30 m. above floor	Pitcher (?); light brown ware, with white grits; *TN* II, Pl. 20: 345; *Beth-zur*, Pl. 11:1.
7	P909	Loc. 103, .14-.57 m. above floor	Rim with circle and triangle design lightly impressed; pink ware, with small white grits; *TN* II, p. 54, Pl. 89:1; *Beth-zur*, Fig. 38; *BASOR*, No. 80, pp. 13-16; *Ramat Rahel*, *IEJ*, Vol. 6, No. 2 Pl. 13:B (Str. IV and V).
8	P1106	Loc. 153, .50 m. above floor	Storage jar; pink ware; *TN* II, Pl. 22:357; *TBM* III, pp. 73 f., 145 f., Pl. 13:8; *Lachish* III, p. 316, Pl. 95:483.
9	P1057	Loc. 135	Handle and shoulder of storage jar; gray ware, with small white grits; see Fig. 32:8.
10	P1056	Loc. 135	Handle and side of storage jar; see Fig. 32:8.
11	P1055	Loc. 135	Storage jar; pinkish-buff ware; see Fig. 32:8.

FIG. 32

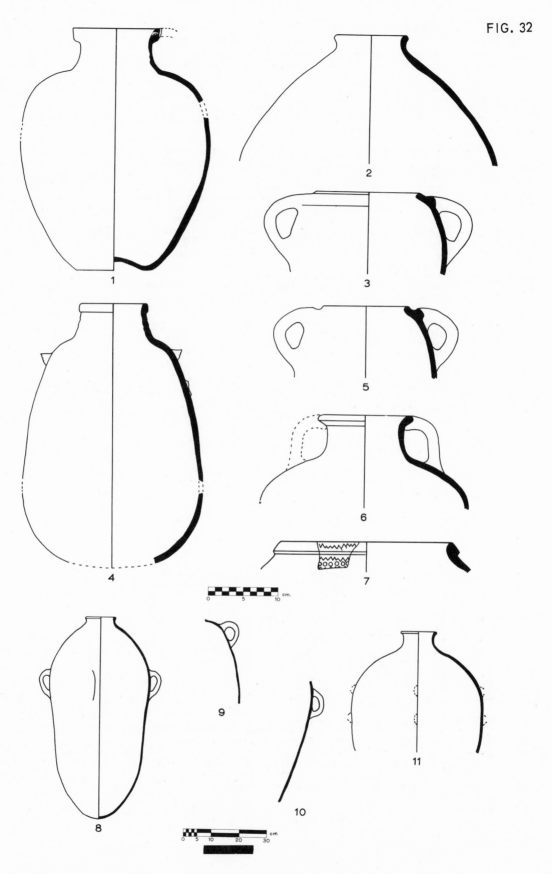

Pottery from Winery

FIGURE 33: POTTERY AND SMALL OBJECTS FROM WINERY

No.	Field No.	Provenience	
1	P958	Loc. 112	Bowl; reddish-brown ware, burnished inside and on outside of rim, with few small grits; cf. *AASOR*, Vol. 34-35, pp. 29-30 Pls. 16A:2, 5, 7, and 22:13-23; *Qasile*, p. 202 f. Pl. 36A:1-14
2	P1336	Loc. 213	Bowl; reddish-brown ware, burnished inside and outside, with mixed grits; *TBM* I, p. 85 f., Pls. 61-65.
3	P1335	Loc. 213	Bowl; reddish-brown ware, burnished inside and on rim, with gray and white grits.
4	P966	Loc. 112, .40 m. above floor	Platter; reddish-brown ware, burnished inside and on rim, with few small white grits; *TBM* III, pp. 131 f., 152 f., Pl. 21:5.
5	P965	Loc. 112, .40 m. above floor	Bowl; reddish-brown ware, burnished inside.
6	P1030	Loc. 135	Bowl; single row of incised holes inside near center; buff ware, gray core, with few small white grits; *TN* II, Pl. 55:1232.
7	P1263	Loc. 212	Lamp; *TBM* I, p. 86 f., Pls. 34:6-10, 70:4, 5, 8, 9, *TBM* III, p. 154, Pl. 69B: 1-11; *Lachish* III, p. 282 f., Pl. 75:16-19.
8	P1258	Loc. 212, .55 m. above floor	Lamp; pinkish-brown ware, with white grits; *Ramat Rahel, IEJ*, Vol. 6, No. 3, Fig. 10:1 (Str. V); *TN* II, Pl. 71:1633-1642
9	P1045	Loc. 137, 1.18-1.51 m. above floor	Lamp; pinkish-buff ware, with white grits.
10	P1249	Loc. 213, .80 m. above floor	Lamp; pinkish-brown ware, with mixed white grits.
11	P967	Loc. 112, .40 m. above floor	Hole-mouth jar with handles; reddish-brown ware, with few white grits; see Fig. 32:3, 5
12	P1338	Loc. 212, .20 m. above floor	Hole-mouth jar; pink ware, with few white grits; *AASOR*, Vol. 34-35, p. 31, Pl. 23:7; *Ramat Rahel, IEJ*, Vol. 6, No. 3, Fig. 10:4 (Str. V).
13	P1039	Loc. 137	Fragment of jar with two concentric rows of triangles deeply impressed; reddish-brown ware, with few grits; *AASOR*, Vol. 34-35, p. 43, Pl. 26:14-16; *Samaria* III, Fig. 32:9a, b, 10; p. 195 (Period VII-VIII).
14	P1029	Loc. 135	Rim of storage jar; pinkish-buff ware, with small white grits; *TBM* III, p. 149, Pl. 17:8.
15	P1084	Loc. 141, .90-1.40 m. above floor	Rim and shoulder of storage jar; pinkish-buff ware, with white grits; *TN* II, Pl. 14:240.
16	P1043	Loc. 137, 1.02-1.18 m. above floor	Funnel; pink ware, with white grits; *TN* I, p. 78, II, pp. 51, 118, 184, Pl. 77:1775-1783; *Gezer* II, p. 185, Fig. 343.
17	P1070	Loc. 135	Jar; pinkish-brown ware, with small white grits; *Lachish* III, Pl. 98:587; *TN* II, Pl. 20:345.
18	P1068	Loc. 135	Rim and shoulder of storage jar; pink ware, with white grits; *TN* II, Pl. 15:264.
19	M64	Loc. 140, .80 m. above floor	Stopper; pink ware, with few small white grits.
20	M65	Loc. 144, 1.20 m. above floor	Bone spatula, fragmentary at end; whitish yellow; polished; *Samaria* III, Fig. 115:4 (Period V); *Lachish* III, Pl. 63:22-27; *TN* I, Pl. 105:26-32.
21	M55	Loc. 112	Scraper made from sherd; coarse surfaces; pink ware, with few small white grits.
22	M35	Loc. 112	Scraper made from sherd; smooth surfaces, burnished on one side; reddish-brown ware, with few small white grits.
23	F20	Loc. 201, .10 m. above floor	Iron blade, badly corroded; *Lachish* III, p. 387.
24	M59	Loc. 139	Bone spatula; brown; polished.
25	M47	Loc. 106, .22-.41 m. above floor.	Bone spatula; tan to gray; polished; *TN* I, p. 272, Pl. 105:26-32; *Lachish*, III, p. 397, Pl. 63:22-27.
26	B59	Loc. 143	Bronze spatula; *TN* I, pp. 265, 272, Pl. 105:2.
27	B85	Loc. 212, .50 m. above floor	Bronze spatula.
28	M107	Loc. 226	Bone spatula, fragmentary at end; light brown; rough on one side, polished on other.
29	M75	Loc. 208	Bone spatula; light brown; polished.
30	B30	Loc. 144, .70 m. above floor	Bronze fibula; spring inserted in bow; clasp fragmentary; pin broken; *Lachish* III, p. 392 f., Pl. 58:20-22; *Gezer* II, p. 79 f.; III Pl. 134:4; *TN* I, pp. 268 f., 281 f., Pl. 111:31.
31	F28	Loc. 216, 1.50 m. above floor	Bronze arrowhead; *Gezer* II, pp. 371 ff., III, Pl. 215:8.
32	F29	Loc. 214, on floor	Iron bowl; two fragmentary projections, possible handle; surfaces oxidized.
33	St71	Loc. 226	Limestone stopper.

FIG. 33

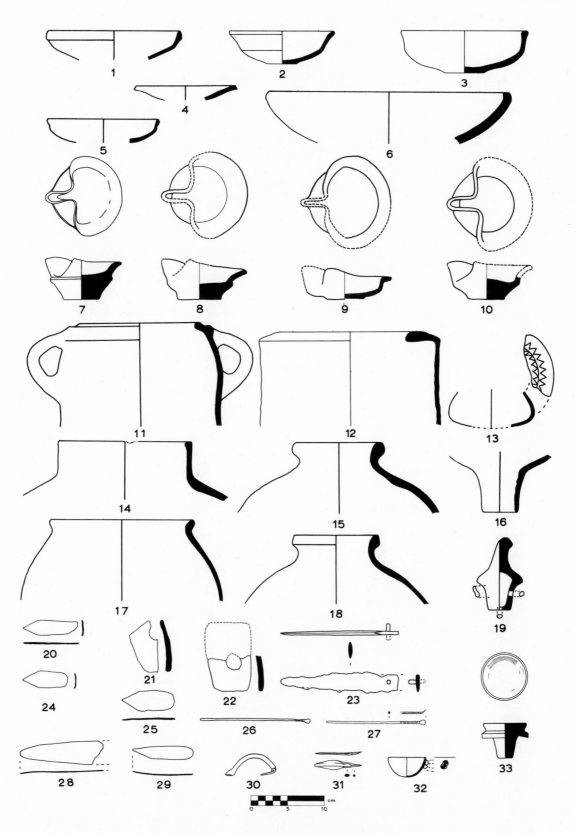

Pottery and Small Objects from Winery

FIGURE 34: POTTERY AND LIMESTONE CUP FROM WINERY

No.	Field No.	Provenience	
1	P1027	Loc. 135	Cooking pot; brown ware, gray core, with large and small white grits; *Beth-zur*, Pl. 10:6; *TBM* I, Pl. 56:8.
2	P1107	Loc. 153	Cooking pot; gray ware; *Lachish* III, Pls. 75:43; 93:449; *Samaria* III, Fig. 12:10 (Period VIII).
3	P1044	Loc. 141	Cooking pot; brown ware, gray core, with white grits; *TN* II, Pl. 50:1051; *TBM* III, Pl. 19:1-4.
4	P1028	Loc. 135, .40-.68 m. above floor	Cooking pot; reddish-brown ware, with few white grits; *Beth-zur*, Pl. 10:2
5	P1026	Loc. 135	Cooking pot; brown ware, with large and small white grits; *Beth-zur*, Pl. 10:6.
6	P1568	Loc. 226	Cooking pot with ribbed body; red ware; *AASOR*, Vol. 29-30, Pl. 23:A173; *AASOR*, Vol. 32-33, Pls. 42:10, 59:1.
7	P1425	Loc. 226	Cooking pot with ribbed body; tan ware; *Samaria* III, Fig. 71:5 (Roman 3a); *Ramat Rahel*, *BIES*, Vol. 24, Fig. 6:15.
8	P1442	Loc. 226	Cooking pot with ribbed body; reddish ware.
9	P1428	Loc. 226	Jug with irregular ribbing; slightly twisted strap handles; light brown ware; *AASOR*, Vol. 29-30, p. 28, Pl. 24:A75.
10	P1495	Loc. 226	Jug with ribbed body; pinkish-white ware; *AASOR*, Vol. 29-30, Pl. 24:A75, A137; *Ramat Rahel*, *BIES*, Vol. 24, Fig. 6: 16, 17.
11	1494	Loc. 226	Jug with ribbed body; cream ware; *Ramat Rahel*, *BIES*, Vol. 24, Fig. 6:26 (Str. IV).
12	P1052	Loc. 141, down 1.40 m.	Juglet; pinkish-buff ware, with few large white grits; handle poorly attached; *Lachish* III, Pl. 89:349.
13	P1196	Loc. 211, .25 m. above floor	Juglet with round mouth; pink ware, light vertical burnishing, with large white grits; *Lachish* III, pp. 294-296, Pl. 73:17, 18; *Samaria* III, Fig. 10:23, 23:12; *TN* II, Pl. 41:781.
14	P1077	Loc. 139, on floor	Bottle with two knob handles; light buff ware with vertical burnishing; light gray core; neck broken and handles slightly chipped; *TN* II, p. 49, Pl. 75:1730; *Lachish* III, Pl. 87: 277.
15	St69	Loc. 226	Limestone cup; white; fluted, chisel marks visible; *AASOR*, Vol. 32-33, Pl. 52:5; *Discoveries in the Judaean Desert II*, Fig. 8:6.

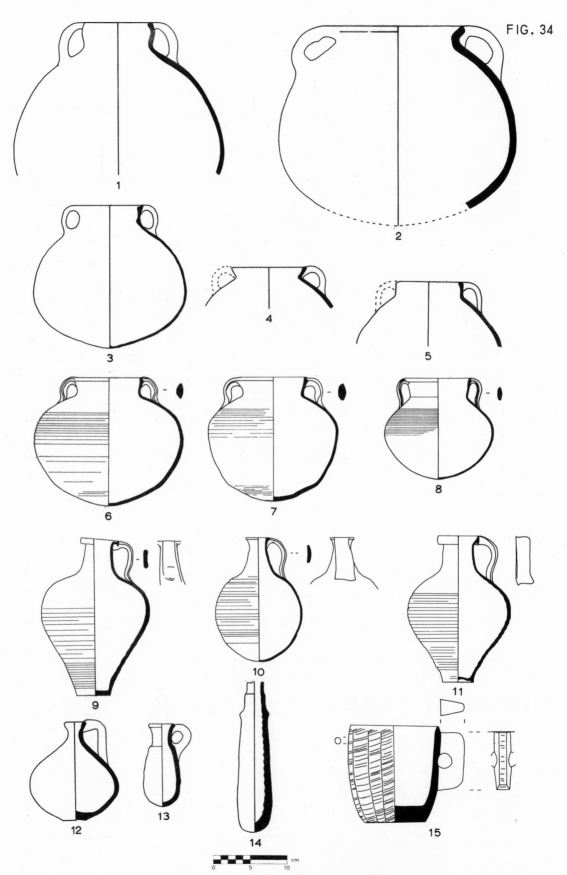

FIG. 34

Pottery and Limestone Cup from Winery

FIGURE 35: POTTERY FROM AREA 10-M-3/4

No.	Field No.	POTTERY FROM EAST OF WALL 2
1	P3384	Lamp with high base, most of flange and nozzle missing, wheel marks inside; reddish-brown ware, dark core; traces of burning on flange.
2	P3383	Cooking pot rim, flanged with one indentation on edge, upper attachment for handle on rim; red ware, well levigated; traces of carbon on rim.
3	P3359	Bowl rim, folded outside; red ware, few white grits; wheel-burnished inside and outside.
4	P3381	Hole-mouth jar rim, folded outside; pinkish-buff ware, gray core, with many small white grits; join of folding of rim apparent on outside.
5	P3382	Bowl rim; buff ware, few small white grits.
5a	P3360	Juglet mouth, neck and part of handle; pinkish-buff ware.
6	P3358	Hole-mouth jar rim, inverted; buff ware, gray core, white grits.
7	P3357	Hole-mouth jar rim, hump down center; pink ware, white grits.
8	P3355	Hole-mouth jar rim, sharp shoulder; reddish-brown ware, white grits.
9	P3354	Hole-mouth jar rim, sharp shoulder; red ware, white grits.
10	P3356	Hole-mouth jar rim, sharp shoulder; reddish-brown ware, white grits.

POTTERY FROM WEST OF WALL 2, ON FLOOR 2

No.	Field No.	
11	P3411	Storage jar, rim folded, two indentations below fold-line outside; reddish-brown ware, large white grits, gray core.
12	P3410	Storage jar, flanged rim, two ridges on collar; reddish-brown ware, white grits, gray core.
13	P3408	Storage jar, flanged rim with ridge on collar; reddish-brown ware, white grits, gray core.
14	P3409	Storage jar, flanged rim, ridge on collar, double fold (?); brown ware, white grits.
15	P3403	Storage jar, folded rim; reddish-brown ware, large white grits, dark core.
16	P3407	Storage jar, flanged rim, ridge on collar; buff ware.
17	P3402	Storage jar, flanged rim, ridge on collar; reddish-brown ware.
18	P3404	Storage jar rim, folded to inside, slight ledge outside; reddish-brown ware, white grits.
19	P3406	Platter rim, beveled and inverted; reddish-brown ware, white grits.

POTTERY FROM MAKE-UP OF FLOOR 2

No.	Field No.	
20	P3309	Jug shoulder, sharp edge; reddish-brown ware, large white grits; cream slip outside decorated with three stripes of paint, outer ones brown, center one red.
21	P3308	Bowl with ring base and carinated shoulder; gray ware, white grits; cream slip outside, burnished.
22	P3307	Large bowl rim; buff ware, white grits.
23	P3251	Bowl rim, incised with deep ridge cutting; red ware.
24	P3306	Jar rim; reddish-brown ware, large white grits.
25	P3305	Cooking pot rim; red ware, large white grits; black deposit on outside.

102

FIG. 35

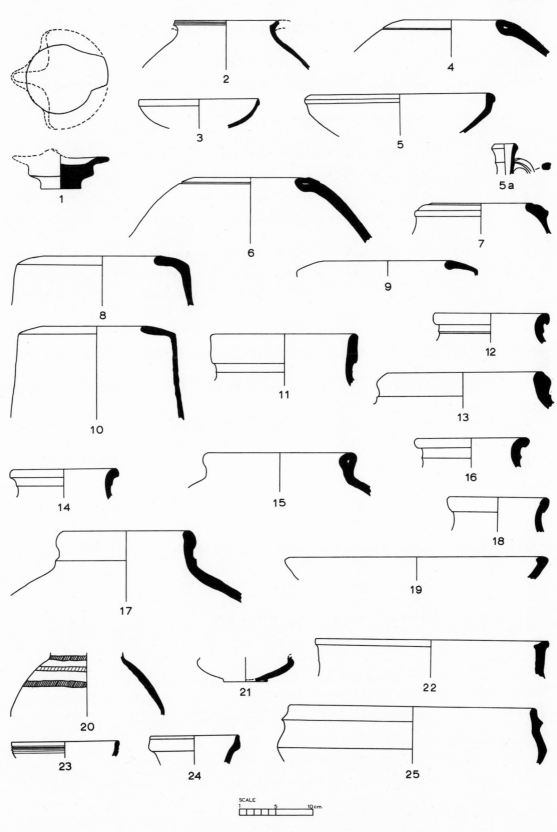

Pottery from Area 10-M-3/4

FIGURE 36: POTTERY FROM AREAS 10-M-3/4, 10-L-5, AND 10-N-4

No.	Field No.	POTTERY FROM FLOOR 3 OF 10-M-3/4
1	P3500	Bowl rim with ridge down center; buff ware; cream slip, burnished on wheel, hatching on shoulder.
2	P3475	Bowl with plain rim; buff ware, dark core; lip painted red and red dots on shoulder.
3	P3343	Jug rim; pinkish-buff ware; black deposit on rim and neck.
4	P3341	Cooking pot rim; brown ware, large white grits; black deposit outside.
5	P3473	Bowl rim; reddish brown ware, dark core.
6	P3474	Jug rim; brown ware, highly burnished outside, vertically on body, horizontally on rim.
8	P3342	Jug rim, folded (?); reddish-brown ware, well levigated.

POTTERY FROM ROOM ADJOINING CITY WALL IN 10-L-5

7	P3449	Rim from bowl or cooking pot; reddish-brown ware, white grits, carbon deposit on outside.
9	P3467	Rim of cooking pot; reddish-brown ware, large grits; *AASOR*, Vol. 4, Pl. 25:11.
10	P3450	Storage jar rim; light brown ware, large grits; double ridge on collar; *TN II*, Pl. 2:26.
11	P3464	Rim of bowl; orange-buff ware, large grits, dark core.
12	P3466	Storage jar rim; orange-buff ware, large grits, dark core; *AASOR*, Vol. 4, Pl. 28:24; Vol. 34-35, Pl. 20:4.
13	P3468	Base fragment; orange-buff ware, large grits, dark core.
14	P3465	Rim of crater (?); orange-buff ware, large grits, dark core; *AS IV*, Pl. 60:26.

POTTERY FROM BURNT LAYER IN 10-N-4

15	P3310	Rim of storage jar; reddish-brown ware, dark core, large grits.
16	P3326	Rim of storage jar; reddish-brown ware.
17	P3364	Jug with pinched mouth; dark red ware; *AS IV*, Pl. 60:2 (Str. III); *TN II*, Pl. 32:561. (Amman.)
18	P3328	Rim of cooking pot; reddish ware; carbon deposit; *AASOR*, Vol. 34-35, Pl. 21:8, 9 (Period II).
	P3512	Sherd of orange-buff ware, burnished by hand.
	P3513	Sherd of gray ware, with cream slip, burnished by hand.

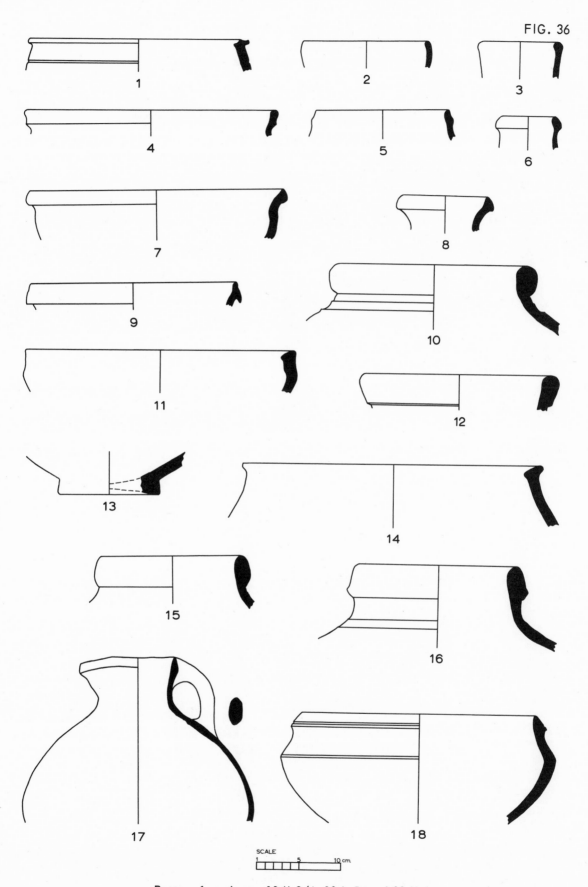

FIG. 36

SCALE

Pottery from Areas 10-M-3/4. 10-L-5, and 10-N-4

FIGURE 37: POTTERY FROM AREA 8-G-6

No.	Field No.	POTTERY FROM PLASTER FLOOR

1 P941 Rim of bowl; grayish-pink ware, burnished on inside and on outside of rim.

2 P942 Rim of bowl; pinkish-buff ware, wet smoothed.

3 P943 Fragment of bowl; gray ware with lighter gray wash; *TBM* I, Pl. 67:9 (A), *Samaria* III, Fig. 10:11 (Period VI).

POTTERY FROM CACHE

4 P853 Bowl with four handles; pinkish-buff ware.

5 P856 Plain bowl without handles.

6 P860 Rim of bowl; red ware.

7 P857 Bowl with four handles; pinkish-buff outside and pinkish-orange inside.

8 P861 Rim of bowl; brownish-pink, ring burnished inside and on rim.

9 P859 Deep cooking pot with two handles; buff ware; *TBM* I, Pl. 56:7 (end of 7th cent.); *TN* II, Pl. 50: 1067.

10 P855 Bowl with four handles; brownish-red ware, ring-burnished on inside and on top of rim.

FIG. 37

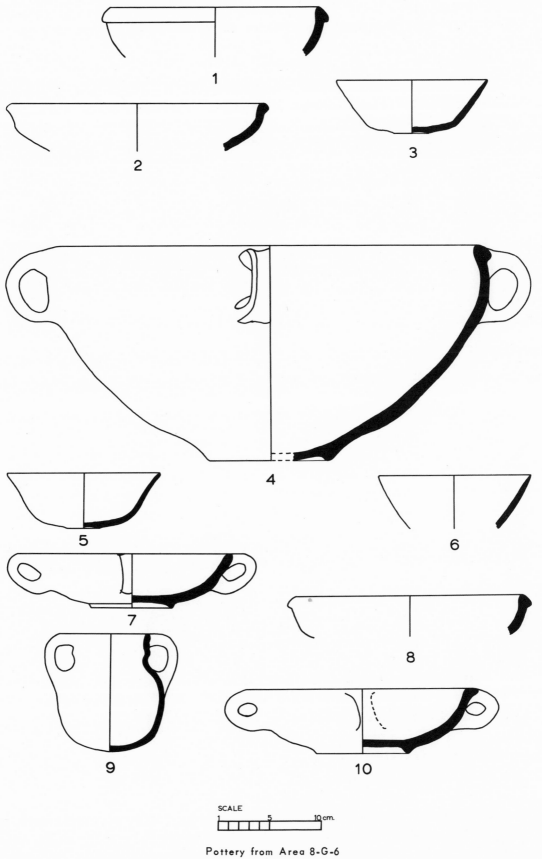

SCALE

Pottery from Area 8-G-6

FIGURE 38: POTTERY AND STONE CUP FROM TRENCH I

No.	Field No.	Provenience	
1	P167	M, on bedrock	Juglet, part of rim and neck missing; red ware, light brown core, traces of cream slip, small white grits; *Samaria* III, Fig. 23:12.
2	P311	L, .30 m. below surface	Hole-mouth jar, portion of rim and shoulder; buff to pink ware, few small white grits; *Lachish* III, Pl. 97:540, p. 316.
3	P335	L, Stratum 2	Small bowl, portion of rim and body; reddish-brown ware, burnished inside and on rim, small gray and white grits, *Lachish* III, Pl. 80:70, p. 277.
4	P61	L, Stratum 2	Bowl, portion of rim and body; buff ware, cream slip, burnished (?), very few grits.
5	P261	J, Stratum 2	Cooking pot, portion of rim; brown ware, black core, many large crystalline grits, traces of burning; *Samaria* III, Fig. 1:22.
6	P55	K, Stratum 2	Cooking pot; reddish-brown ware, gray core, white and crystalline grits, traces of burning; *TN* II, Pl. 50:1059.
7	P312	L, .30 m. below surface	Large bowl, portion of rim and body; buff to pink ware, black and white grits; *TBM* III, Pl. 20:2.
8	P206	H, Stratum 2	Large storage jar, portion of rim and body; buff ware, gray core, large and small grits.
9	P240	J, Stratum 2	Large shallow bowl, portion of rim and body; pink to buff ware, light gray core, small white grits.
10	P62	L, Stratum 2	Hole-mouth jar, portion of rim; red ware, gray core, few white grits; *Lachish* III, Pl. 97:552, p. 319
11	P50	K, Stratum 2	Lamp, part of rim missing; buff ware, gray core, large and small white grits; *Lachish* III, Pl. 83:150, p. 285.
12	P45	K, Loc. 1	Cooking pot, portion of rim, handles and body; reddish-brown ware, dark gray core, few white grits; *AASOR*, Vol. 32-33, Pl. 59:1.
13	P34	J, Bin	Large jar, portion of rim and body; pinkish-buff ware, light gray core, small white grits.
14	St12	K-L, Stratum 1	Stone cup, handle with portion of rim and body; carved limestone, smooth inside, vertical cutting outside, chisel marks on handle; *Discoveries in the Judaean Desert* II, Fig. 8:6.
15	P222	J, 1 m. below surface	Juglet, repaired; light red ware, cream slip, strap handle slightly twisted; *Discoveries in the Judaean Desert* II, Fig. 8:10.
16	P43/ 273	K, Loc. 1	Large jar, portion of rim, neck and body; pink ware, gray core, cream slip, few small white grits; *AASOR*, Vol. 32-33, Pl. 58:29.
17	P346	M, Bath	Juglet, portion of rim, neck and body; reddish-brown ware, dark gray core, few small white grits.
18	P355	M, Bath	Nozzle of lamp, bowed spout; gray ware, knife-cut surface; *AASOR*, Vol. 32-33, Pl. 59:33.
19	P347	M, Bath	Large jar, portion of rim, neck and body; light brown ware, light gray core, few white grits; *AASOR*, Vol. 32-33, Pl. 58:32
20	P251	J, .70 m. below surface	Shallow bowl, base with portion of body and rim; reddish-brown ware, small white grits; *AASOR*, Vol. 29-30, Pl. 23:A81.
21	P255	J, .70 m. below surface	Juglet, neck and handle with portion of rim and body; red ware, cream slip on outside extending into neck, few white grits; *AASOR*, Vol. 29-30, Pl. 24:X23.
22	P46	K, Loc. 1	Lentoid flask, rim, neck and portion of twisted handles; light brown ware, gray core, small white grits, neck made separate from body; *AASOR*, Vol. 32-33, Pl. 59:35.

FIG. 38

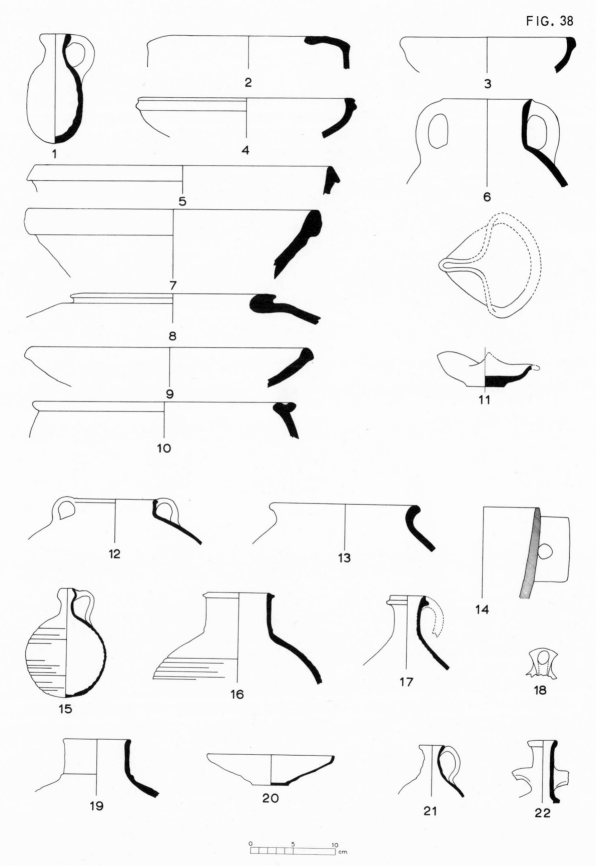

Pottery and Stone Cup from Trench I

FIGURE 39: POTTERY FROM LEVEL 1 OF AREA 15-K-18

No.

1   Portion of rim and body of bowl; buff ware with gray core; many small white grits.

2   Portion of rim of hole-mouth jar; dark pinkish-buff ware; small white and few dark grits.

3   Portion of rim of bowl; light brown ware.

4   Portion of rim and body of bowl; light brown ware burnished inside.

5   Portion of rim of bowl; reddish-brown ware with cream slip burnished inside and on rim; white grits.

6   Portion of rim of bowl; pinkish-buff ware; small white grits.

7   Portion of rim, body, and handle of crater; reddish-brown ware, dark gray core, burnished inside and on rim and upper part of handle; large and small white grits.

8   Portion of rim and body of bowl; reddish-brown ware burnished inside and on rim; large and small white grits; burning on outside.

9   Portion of rim, body, and handle of crater; reddish-brown ware with dark gray core; burnished on rim, inside, and upper part of handle; large and small white grits.

10 Portion of rim of bowl; reddish-brown ware with gray core, burnished on rim and inside; white grits.

11 Portion of rim and body of bowl; light brown ware, burnished inside and on rim; small white grits.

12 Portion of rim and neck of jar; dark pinkish-buff ware with brown core; many small white grits.

13 Portion of rim of hole-mouth jar; buff ware with gray core; many small white grits.

14 Portion of rim of bowl; reddish-brown ware with gray core, burnished on rim and inside; white grits.

15 Portion of rim and body of jar; buff ware; many small white grits.

16 Portion of rim and body of hole-mouth jar; dark pinkish-buff ware with cream slip; many large and small white grits.

17 Portion of rim of crater; dark gray ware with light greenish slip, burnished on rim and inside; many large and small white grits.

18 Portion of rim and neck of jar; pinkish-buff ware; many small white grits.

19 Portion of rim and neck of jar; dark reddish-brown ware; traces of burning.

20 Portion of rim and neck of storage jar; buff ware; small white grits.

21 Portion of rim and neck of storage jar; buff ware with black core; many small white grits.

22 Base of bowl; light brown ware; few dark grits.

23 Portion of shoulder and body of jug; reddish-brown ware with dark gray core, cream slip; large and small white grits.

24 Lamp with part of rim missing; light brown ware; few white and dark grits; burning on spout.

25 Portion of rim and neck of jar; buff ware; small white grits.

26 Portion of rim and neck of storage jar; dark pinkish-buff ware with brown core; many small white grits.

27 Portion of base and side of ring stand; buff ware; large and small white grits.

FIG. 39

LEVEL 1   15 - K - 18

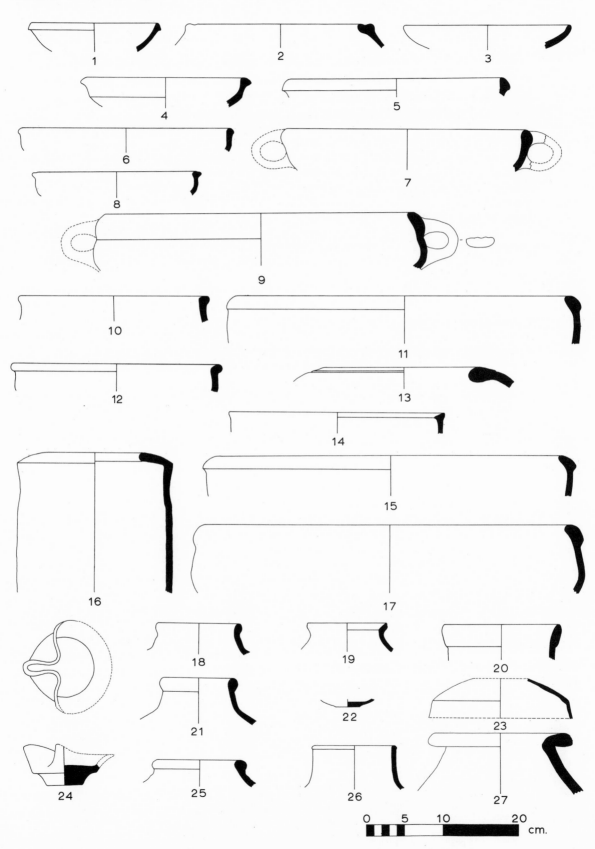

Pottery from Level 1 of Area 15-K-18

FIGURE 40: POTTERY AND GRINDSTONE FROM LEVEL 3 OF AREA 15-K-18

No.

1 Fragment of rim and wall of bowl; buff ware burnished inside and on rim spirally; red and white grits.

2 Fragment of rim of jar; pink ware burnished inside and on rim; white grits.

3 Ring base; buff ware with red slip burnished outside; black grits.

4 Fragment of rim and handle; buff ware; large brown and white grits.

5 Fragment of rim and wall of bowl; red to buff ware burnished inside and on rim spirally, black and white grits.

6 Fragment of rim of jar; buff to pink ware burnished inside and on rim; white grits.

7 Rim of jug with handle (probably only one); dark reddish-brown ware; black and white grits.

8 Fragment of rim of jar; light brown ware; gray and white grits.

9 Fragment of rim of jar; buff ware; black and white grits.

10 Fragment of rim of jar; light brown ware; red and white grits.

11 Fragment of shoulder of bowl; buff ware with red slip burnished outside; black grits.

12 (M90) Grindstone; central hole, bored from both sides; basalt.

13 Fragment of rim of jar; pinkish-buff ware; small white grits.

14. Fragment of rim of pot with handle; dark reddish-brown ware.

FIG. 40

LEVEL 3   15 - K - 18

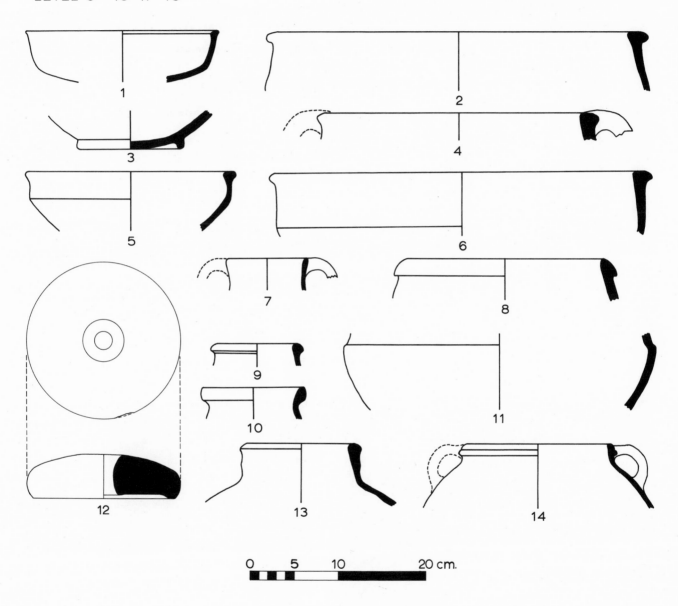

Pottery and Grindstone from Level 3 of Area 15-K-18

FIGURE 41: POTTERY AND STONE FROM LEVEL 4a OF AREA 15-K-18

No.

1   Fragment of ring base; light brown ware with cream slip outside, wheel burnished; white grits; possibly part of No. 13.

2   Fragment of ring base; wheel marks on base; buff ware; white grits.

3   Fragment of rim of bowl; brown ware; white grits.

4   Fragment of rim of storage jar; combing on shoulder; buff to pink ware; white grits.

5   Fragment of rim of storage jar; pinkish-buff ware; black and white grits.

6   Fragment of rim of storage jar; gray ware; white grits.

7   Fragment of rim of storage jar; buff ware; brown and white grits.

8   Fragment of rim of cooking pot; dark reddish-brown ware; large white grits; blackened on outside; *TBM* Ia, Pl. 13: 10.

9   Fragment of rim of storage jar; buff ware; small white grits.

10 Fragment of rim of storage jar; gray ware; small white grits.

11 Fragment of rim of storage jar; combing on shoulder; light red ware.

12 Fragment of rim and wall of cooking pot; brown ware; large grits; *TBM* Ia, Pl. 13: 9 (D).

13 Fragment of shoulder of jar; light brown ware with cream slip; wheel burnished, white grits; pattern of incised lines along shoulder; *TBM* I, Pl. 41: 13 (D).

Other fragments of same jar (not illustrated): (13a) Piece of shoulder; light brown ware with cream slip; white grits; incised lines. (13b) Piece of shoulder; light brown ware; white grits; incised lines. (13c) Piece of shoulder; light brown ware with cream slip; burnished pattern of horizontal lines. (13d) Piece of shoulder; light buff ware with cream slip; burnished pattern of horizontal lines.

14 Handle of jar; light brown ware; small white grits.

15 Fragment of rim of jar; buff ware; small white grits.

16 Fragment of rim of storage jar; light brown ware.

17 Handle with raised center section and fragment of wall of jar; light brown with cream slip burnished; very small white grits.

18 Handle and fragment of wall of jar; light brown ware.

19 Side and handle of cooking pot; coarse brown ware; large grits; *TBM* Ia, Pl. 13: 9 (D).

20 (St. 66) Rubbing or grinding stone; gray.

FIG. 41

LEVEL 4a 15 - K - 18

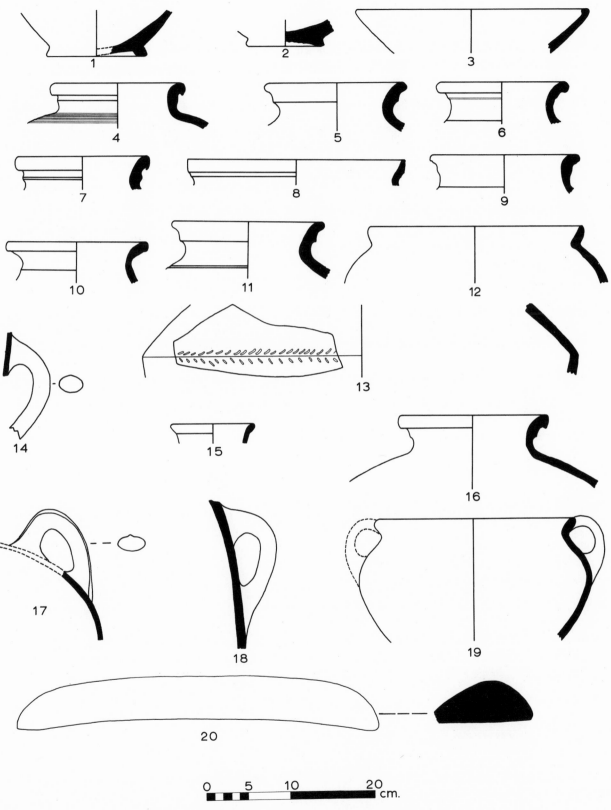

Pottery and Stone from Level 4a of Area 15-K-18

FIGURE 42: POTTERY FROM LEVEL 4b OF AREA 15-K-18

No.

1   Fragment of rim; brown ware with cream slip; small black and white grits.

2   Fragment of rim of cooking pot; light red ware; crystalline and gray grits; band of indented decoration below rim; *TBM* Ia, Pl. 13: 5 (D).

3   Ring base; light brown ware with cream slip outside, burnished; white grits.

4   Base of sharply carinated bowl with ring base recessed on inside; light brown ware; cream slip outside, burnished; small white grits.

5   Fragment of rim of cooking pot; light brown ware; large grits; incised rope pattern below rim; fragment too small to get exact angle; *TBM* Ia, Pl. 13: 4 (D).

6   Fragment of rim of bowl; red ware.

7   Fragment of rim of bowl; buff ware; small black and white grits.

8   Fragment of shoulder of storage jar; gray ware; small white grits; pattern of combing.

9   Fragment of wall of juglet with handle; burnished; red ware with gray core; small white grits.

10   Fragment of rim of bowl; pinkish-buff ware; white grits.

11   Fragment of rim of pedestal vase (?); wheel-burnished on inside as well as on outside; light brown ware; small white grits; *Bronze Age Cemetery*, Fig. 26: 2.

12   Fragment of rim of storage jar; buff ware; small black and white grits; *TBM* Ia, Pl. 14: 5, 10 (D).

13   Fragment of shoulder of storage jar; light brown ware; small white grits; pattern of combing.

14   Fragment of rim of storage jar; buff ware; small black and white grits.

15   Fragment of rim of storage jar; pink ware with gray core; small white grits.

16   Sherd; gray ware; white crystalline grits.

17   Fragment of handle and wall; red ware with cream to pink slip, hand burnished; brown and white grits; horizontal wheel marks inside.

18   Fragment of wall of storage jar; light brown ware with cream slip, burnished outside; white grits.

FIG. 42

LEVEL 4b 15 - K - 18

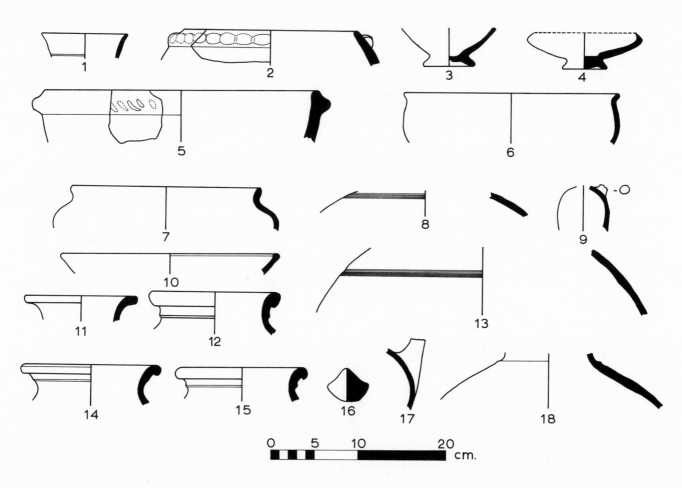

Pottery from Level 4b of Area 15-K-18

FIGURE 43: POTTERY AND OTHER ARTIFACTS FROM LEVEL 1 OF AREA 15-L-18

No.

1   Portion of rim and body of bowl; reddish-brown ware with light brown core, burnished inside and on rim; small white grits.

2   Portion of rim of dish; reddish-brown ware burnished inside; white grits.

3   Portion of rim and body of bowl; reddish-brown ware with traces of burnishing on rim and inside; white grits; burned on inside.

4   Portion of rim and side of bowl; buff to pink ware with brown core, slight traces of burnishing on rim and inside; many small white grits.

5   Portion of rim and body of bowl; dark buff ware; many small white grits.

6   Portion of rim of crater; buff ware with traces of burnishing inside and on rim.

7   Portion of rim and body of bowl; reddish-brown ware burnished inside and on rim; few small white grits.

8   Portion of rim and side of bowl; dark pinkish-buff ware with light brown core, traces of burnishing on rim and inside; some dark and white grits.

9   Portion of rim and body of crater; light brown ware with light gray core; small white grits.

10   Portion of rim and shoulder with handle of crater; buff ware with brown core, small white grits.

11   Portion of rim of hole-mouth jar; pink ware with brown core, cream slip; many small white grits.

12   Portion of rim of crater; reddish-brown ware with gray core, traces of burnishing on rim; large white grits.

13   Portion of rim of hole-mouth jar; pink ware with brown core, cream slip; small white grits.

14   Portion of rim of hole-mouth jar; pink to buff ware with brown core; small white grits.

15   Portion of rim and neck of jar; reddish-brown ware with gray core; few small white grits.

16   Portion of rim and neck of jar; pinkish-buff ware with gray core; many small white grits.

17   Portion of rim, neck, and shoulder of jar; buff ware; small white grits.

18   Portion of rim, neck, and shoulder of jar; light gray ware with gray core; few dark and white grits.

19   Portion of rim, neck and handle of juglet; buff ware; few small white grits.

20   Handle of jug; buff ware; small white grits.

21   Bone spatula.

22   (B117) Bronze arrowhead; three-flanged blade, socketed.

23   (B62) Bronze rod; end square in section; four tooth-like projections.

FIGURE 44: POTTERY FROM LEVEL 2 OF AREA 15-L-18

No.

1   Fragment of rim of large jar; reddish-buff ware with gray core; white grits.

2   Rim of hole-mouth jar; pinkish-buff ware; red and white grits.

3   Fragment of rim of large jar; buff ware; small white grits.

4   Juglet, without neck; red ware with red slip burnished; white grits.

5   (P1194) Rim of bowl; pinkish-buff ware; small black grits.

6   Juglet; red ware.

7   Fragment of lamp; light reddish-brown ware; black grits; burned at spout.

LEVEL 1 15 - L - 18

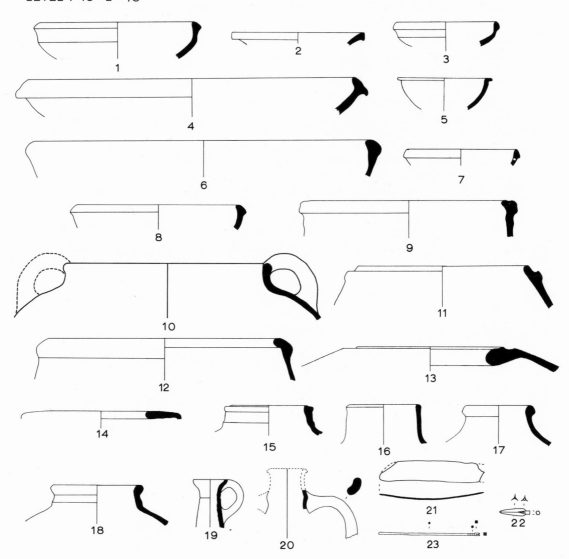

Fig.43. Pottery and Other Artifacts from Level 1 of Area 15-L-18

LEVEL 2 15 - L - 18

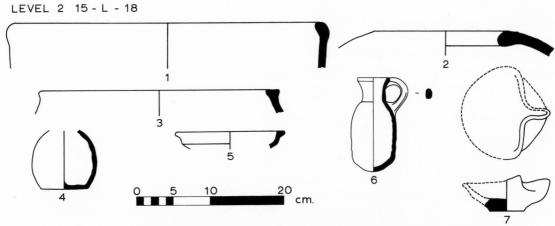

Fig.44. Pottery from Level 2 of Area 15-L-18

FIGURE 45: POTTERY FROM LEVEL 3 OF AREA 15-L-18

No.

1   Fragment of rim of bowl; pinkish-buff ware; white grits.

2   Fragment of ring base; light brown ware; white grits.

3   Fragment of rim of bowl; pinkish-buff ware; small white grits.

4   Fragment of rim of bowl; light brown ware with gray core; white grits.

5   Fragment of rim of bowl; light brown ware discolored; white grits.

6   Fragment of handle; pinkish-buff ware; red and white grits.

7   Fragment of rim of jar; pink ware; small white grits.

8   Fragment of rim of storage jar; buff ware with gray core; brown grits.

FIGURE 46: POTTERY AND LOOM WEIGHT FROM LEVEL 4 OF AREA 15-L-18

No.

1   Fragment of wall and handle of storage jar; buff ware; small white grits.

2   Fragment of wall of jar; buff ware; small white grits; combing.

3   Ring base; light brown ware; buff slip outside.

4   Fragment of ring base; buff slip outside, burnished; buff ware; white grits.

5   Fragment of rim of jar with handle; light brown ware; buff slip; white grits.

6   Fragment of rim of storage jar; light brown ware; small white grits.

7   Loom weight of clay.

8   Juglet with twin handle; reddish brown ware; small white grits.

LEVEL 3 15 - L - 18

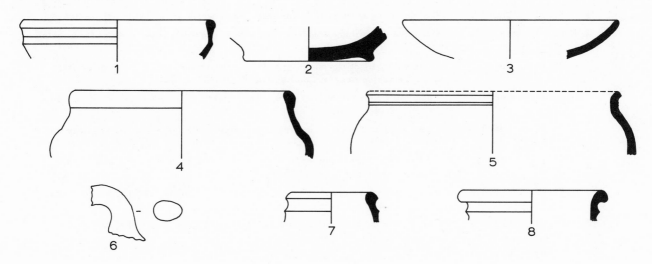

Fig.45. Pottery from Level 3 of Area 15-L-18

LEVEL 4 15 - L - 18

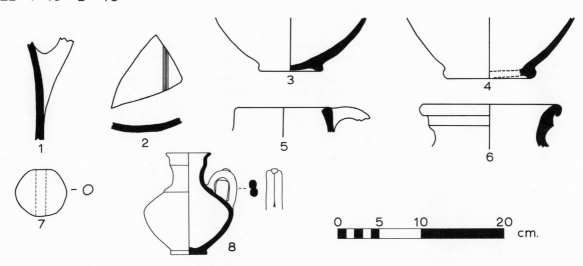

Fig.46. Pottery and Loom Weight from Level 4 of Area 15-L-18

FIGURE 47: POTTERY AND STONE JAR FROM HOUSES IN AREA 17

No.	Field No.	Provenience	
1	P1054	Loc. 122	Portion of rim and body of shallow bowl; reddish-brown ware, dark reddish-brown slip, burnished inside and on rim, with few white grits; *Lachish* III, Pl. 101:626.
2	P1022	Loc. 121	Part of ring stand; buff ware, light gray core, with small white grits; hole, 4 mm. in diameter, pierced through wall before firing; *TN* II, Pl. 77:1769.
3	P1061	Loc. 122	Rim and neck of large jar; pink ware, many white grits; *TN* II, Pl. 18:306.
4	P1041	Loc. 123	Base and rim of lamp; reddish-brown ware, gray core, few white grits; *Lachish* III, Pl. 83:152, p. 285.
5	P1035	Loc. 124	Lamp with part of rim missing; reddish-brown ware, large and small white grits; smoke on nozzle; *Lachish* III, Pl. 83:151, p. 285.
6	P1031	Loc. 118	Lamp; buff ware, light gray core, small white grits; smoke on nozzle; *Lachish* III, Pl. 83:148, p. 285.
7	P1010	Loc. SW122	Lamp; reddish-brown ware, gray core, large and small white grits; smoke on nozzle; *Lachish* III, Pl. 83:149, p. 285.
8	P1011	Loc. 118	Portion of rim, neck and body of cooking pot; dark brown ware, gray core, white and crystalline grits; *TN* II, Pl. 50:1061.
9	P1015	Loc. 118	Portion of rim, neck, and body of cooking pot; reddish-brown ware, light gray core, with white and crystalline grits; *TN* II, Pl. 50:1061.
10	P1021	Loc. 118	Portion of rim, body and handle of juglet; buff ware, cream slip, few dark grits; *TN* II, Pl. 42:829.
11	P1034	Loc. 124	Rim, neck, handle, and portion of body of pitcher; reddish-brown ware, large and small white grits; *Lachish* III, Pl. 86:238, p. 292.
12	P1009	Loc. 118	Rim and part of body of jug with handle; light brown ware, small white grits.
13	P1059	Loc. 122	Juglet with handle and part of rim missing; pink to buff ware, traces of buff slip, few large and small white grits; *Samaria* III, Fig. 23:11, p. 170.
14	P1071	Loc. 122	Cooking pot with part of body missing; dark brown ware, white and crystalline grits; blackened on body, side, and rim; *TN* II, Pls. 45:955 and 46:975.
15	P1086	Loc. 123	Spout to three-handled jar; reddish-brown ware, white grits; *Lachish* III, Pl. 89:373; *TN* II, Pl. 30:523-527.
16	P1085	Loc. 123	Portion of rim, neck, body, and handle of pitcher; reddish-brown ware, light gray core, few white grits; *Samaria* III, Fig. 22:12.
17	St47	Loc. W121	Part of rim of stone jar; black, green, and white marble; well cut and polished.
18	P1073/ 1074	Loc. SW122	Bottle; reddish-brown ware, reddish-brown slip, burnished, traces of brown paint in horizontal bands on neck and body; *TN* II, Pl. 75:1721.
19	P1032	Loc. W118	Pyxis fragment; light red ware, burnished, few small white grits; two horizontal bands of dark brown paint on body.
20	P1060	Loc. 124	Jug with part of rim and neck missing; buff ware, cream slip, few white and dark grits; *TN* II, Pl. 32:564.

FIG. 47

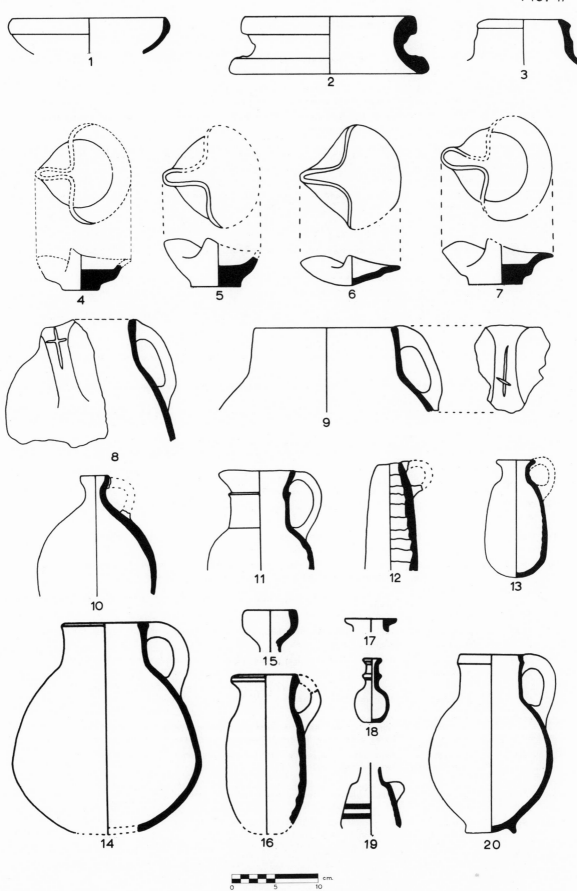

Pottery and Stone Jar from Houses in Area 17

No.	Field No.	Provenience	
1	P1005	Loc. 118, fill above floor	Portion or rim, neck and body of cooking pot; light brown ware, light gray core, white and crystalline grits; *TN* II, Pl. 50:1061.
2	P964	17-G-18, .65 m. down	Part of rim and body of hole-mouth jar; pinkish-buff ware, small white grits, plaster applied to rim; *Lachish* III, Pl. 97:541.
3	P968	17-G-20, 2 m. down	Neck, handle, and part of rim of juglet; pink ware, light gray core, rim horizontally burnished, neck vertically burnished, large and small white grits; handle has central depression; *TN* II, Pl. 39:734.
4	P971	17-H-20, .40 m. below top of bin	Part of rim and body of dish; pinkish-buff ware, small white grits; *Samaria* III, Fig. 11:12.
5	P939	17-G-20, 1.3 m. down	Part of rim and body of bowl; light brown ware, light gray core, small white grits; *Samaria* III, Fig. 11:9.
6	St38	17-H-19, .50 m. down	Cosmetic palette of carved limestone; most of top surface broken away; *TBM* III, Pl. 27:B3.
7	P986	17-G-19, .60 m. down	Neck, handles, and part of body of pilgrim flask; buff ware, pink core, few mixed grits; *TN* II, Pl. 75:1740.
8	P977	17-H-20, .80 m. below top of bin	Sherd; light brown ware, pink slip, small white grits; alternating bands of red and brown paint.
9	P997	17-I-18, .90 m. down	Part of rim and body of bowl; buff ware, white grits, bands of brown and red paint across rim and on inside.
10	P981	17-G-19	Fragment of handle; buff ware, few white and dark grits; three bands of brown paint across handle; smear of pink paint or discoloration on lower part.
11	St41	17/I-18, .95 m. down	Limestone cup; smooth inside, vertical cuttings outside; chisel marks in bottom and on handle.
12	P975	17-G-19, .35 m. down	Lentoid flask; pink ware, with small white grits; neck made separate from body and then attached; *AASOR*, Vol. 32-33, Pl. 59:35.
13	St49	17-F-20, on floor, 1.9 m. down	Dagger pommel; carved gray stone (Amman).
14	P949	17-G-20, 1.7 m. down	Handmade juglet; light brown ware, gray core, few large white grits; horizontal band of brown paint on body.
15	P962	17-G-20, 1.8 m. down	Part of rim and neck of jar; light brown ware, gray core, black grits; *AASOR*, Vol. 4, Pl. 28:11.
16	P973	17-G-19, .25 m. down	Funnel; pinkish-buff ware, light gray core, few white grits.
17	P980	17-H-20, .80 m. below top of bin	Storage jar; reddish-buff ware, few white and dark grits; decoration of wedges and circles on rim and on body above handle.
18	B43	17-H-19, surface	Bronze fibula; *TN* I, Pl. 110:23, 27, 29 (Amman).
19	P959	17-G-18, 1.3 m. down	Juglet; light red ware, burnished and painted with two horizontal bands of brown paint (Amman).
20	B37	17-G-20, .80 m. down	Bronze arrowhead; flat blade, point broken, square tang (Amman).
21	P1037	17-F-19, 1.75 m. down	Rim and neck of storage jar; light brown ware, dark gray core; with large dark and white grits; *AASOR*, Vol. 34-35, Pl. 20:4, 18.
22	P984	17-G-19, .60 m. down	Storage jar; pinkish-buff ware, gray core, few small white grits; decoration of wedge-shaped impressions on rim and on body below neck; three holes pierced in neck and body after firing; *Lachish* III, Pl. 91:405.
23	B48	17-H-20, .90 m. below top of bin	Bracelet-like object of bronze; flat section on top, round on sides, ends twisted together.
24	F12	17-G-19, .20 m. down	Sickle blade, tang and point broken; corroded iron.
25	St36	17-H-20, .55 m. down	Pottery stamp seal; buff ware, gray core, few white grits; longitudinal cutting marks on surface.

124

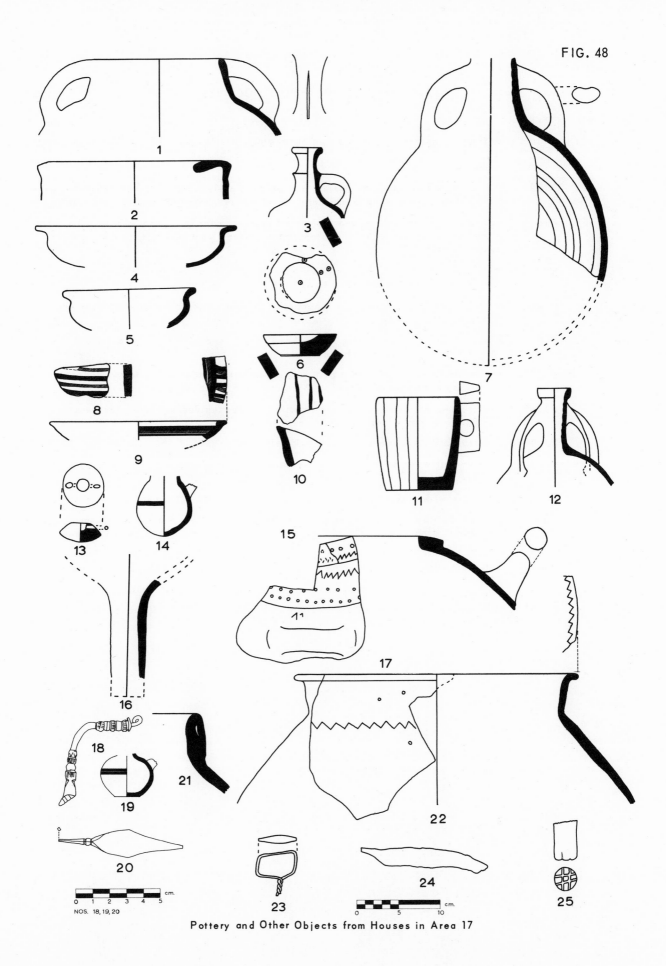

FIG. 48

Pottery and Other Objects from Houses in Area 17

NOS. 18, 19, 20

FIGURE 49: LAMPS FROM LOC. 138

No.	Field No.	
1	P1100	Buff ware; molded bottom has ring base with potter's mark of a "V" in the center; top molded with volutes and ribbing; cf. Karm al-Shaikh, *QDAP*, Vol. 1, Pl. 6:11 (upper left).
2	P1090	Pinkish-buff ware; top and bottom molded separately; ring base; top decorated with volutes and panels of horizontal and vertical lines; traces of dark brown paint.
3	P1091	Buff ware; molded bottom and top joined before firing; ring base with potter's mark of cross with curved ends in center; top decorated with two volutes and border of concentric circles.
4	P1092	Buff ware, with dark brown paint on upper half; top and bottom molded separately; low ring base; top decorated with volutes and triangles.
5	P1047	Pinkish-buff ware; bottom and top molded separately; decoration of volutes and circles on upper part.
6	P1094	Pinkish-buff ware; ring base; herringbone design and volutes on shoulder; dark paint on both inside and outside.
7	P1101	Pinkish-buff ware with brown paint on upper portion; top and bottom molded separately; ring base; top decorated with volutes and hatched design.
8	P1089	Buff ware with traces of dark brown paint on top; top and bottom molded separately; ring base; design on top unclear.
9	P1049	Pinkish-buff ware; fragments of black paint.
10	P1099	Pinkish-buff ware, with dark brown paint on top side; ring base; decoration on top not clear.
11	P1048	Buff ware with pink tinge; brown paint; herringbone design on top.
12	P1102	Buff ware with traces of brown paint; upper and lower parts molded separately; volutes and herringbone design on top (cf. No. 6, which could have been from same mold); ring base; *Samaria* III, Fig. 88:10.
	P1095	Buff ware with black paint; ring base; design on top effaced; 7.9 by 6.4 by 2.2 cm.
	P1075	Light buff ware, painted black inside and outside; ring base; design on top abraded.
	P1093	Pinkish-buff ware, with dark brown paint inside and outside; flat base.

FIG. 49

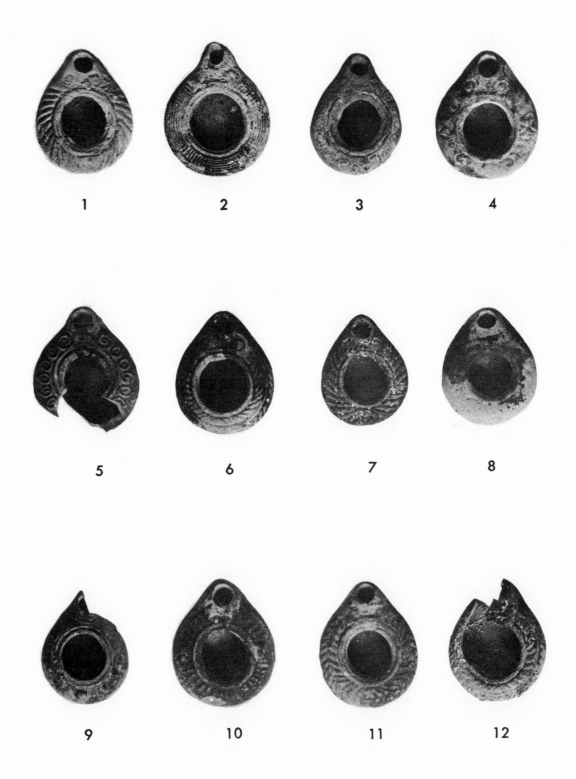

Lamps from Loc. 138

FIGURE 50: OBJECTS FROM WINERY AREAS

No.	Field No.	Provience	
1	B76	Loc. 201, .70 m. above floor	Bronze statuette; spiked base broken at tip; length, 10.5 cm.
2	St34	Loc. 113	Stone weight; tapering toward top; uneven rounded bottom; 15.5 cm. high, 15.5 cm. wide, 3.5 cm. thick at top, and 11.5 cm. thick at bottom.
3	S514	S of Loc. 139, 1 m. down	Basalt stamp seal; rounded top, pierced by hole, .5 cm. in diameter, at mid-point through side; 3.2 cm. high; 3.6 cm. diameter at base; *Gezer II*, Fig. 437:6; *Gezer III*, Pl. 200:9; S.S. Weinberg, ed. *The Aegean and the Near East*, Pl. 18:a.
4	S511	Loc. 136, 1.20-1.40 m. above floor	Stamp impression on single-ridge handle; buff ware, with mixed grits; 2.2 by 1.6 cm; *Hebrew Inscriptions*, p. 27.
5	B56	Loc. 137	Tweezers of bronze; 5.6 cm. long; *Samaria III*, Fig. 104:1, 2; *TN I*, Pl. 105:13, 14.
6	Pfig. 139	Loc. 149, 1.9 m. above floor	Horse's head; pink ware; hollow inside, probably spout; 5 by 4 cm.; *TN II*, p. 52, Pl. 78: 1797.
7	S512	Loc. 136, 1.20-1.40 m. above floor	Stamp impression on single-ridge handle; buff ware with mixed grits; 3.2 by 1.6 cm.

FIG. 50

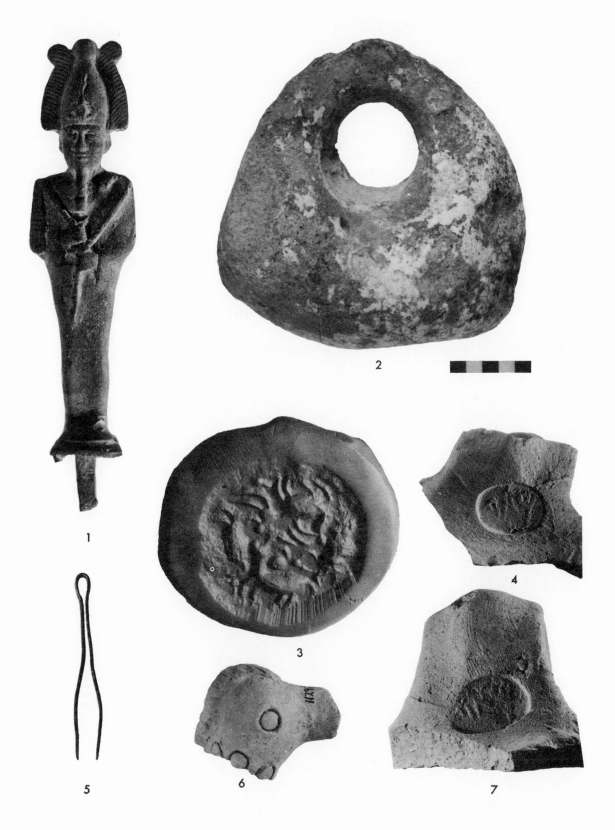

1

2

3

4

5

6

7

Objects from Winery Areas

FIGURE 51: OBJECTS FROM HOUSES IN AREA 17

No.	Field No.	Provenience	
1	F13	17-G-18, 1.65 m. below surface	Iron sickle blade, broken.
2	S496	17-G-19, .75 m. below surface	Stamped jar handle, broken; single ridge; light brown ware, gray core, large white grits; royal stamp Type III; *mlk* above figure.
3	M56	Loc. 123	Bone blade, broken.
4	S504	17-G-18, 1.65 m. below surface	Stamped jar handle; single ridge; reddish-brown ware, gray core, large white grits; royal stamp Type III; concentric circles.
5	B39	17-G-20, 1.50 m. below surface	Bronze arrowhead, square tang.
6	S495	17-H-19, .40 m. below surface	Stamped jar handle; single rounded ridge; buff ware, dark and light grits, oval seal stamped at junction of handle and body; *m* and part of *s* visible.
7	B53	Loc. 118	Bronze needle.
8	B44	17-H-20, .80 m. below top of bin	Bronze spatula, no design.
9	B41	17-H-20, .40 m. below top of bin	Bronze spatula, tip broken, no design.
10	M52	17-G-19, .70 m. below surface	Bone awl.
11	B46	17-H-20, .80 m. below top of bin	Bronze spatula, broken.
12	B45	17-H-20, .80 m. below top of bin	Two thin overlapping sheets of bronze riveted together with small rivets; one large rivet near left center.
13	S515	17-F-19, 2.30 m. below surface	Stamped jar handle; single rounded ridge; reddish-brown ware, gray core, large white grits; royal seal Type II; *mlk* visible above figure; part of *m* below; stamped upside down.
14-16	S494	17-H-20, .80 m. below top of bin	Stamp seal, light gray translucent stone; octagonal convex base, pierced domed top, (Amman).

FIG. 51

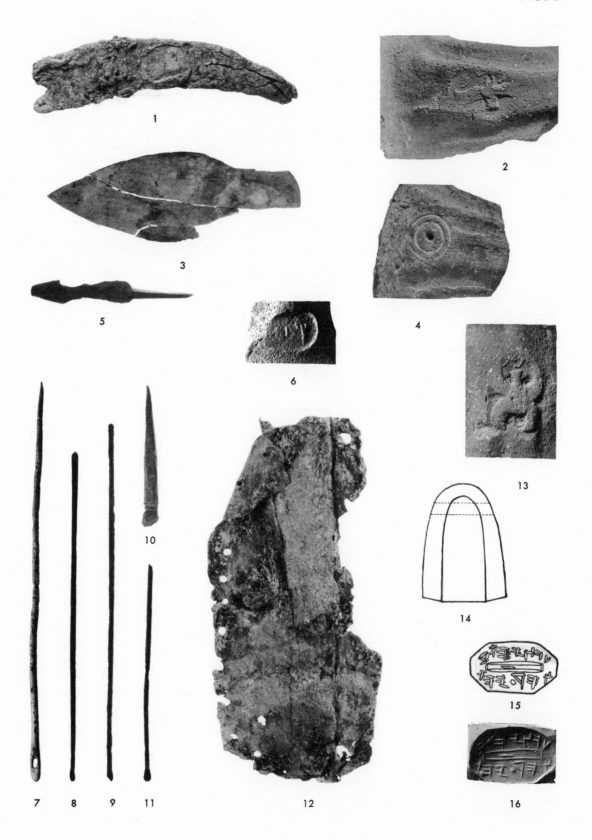

Objects from Houses in Area 17

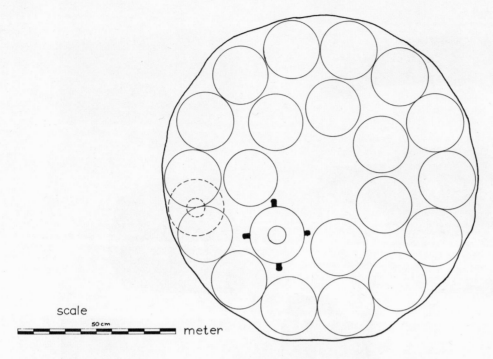

scale
50 cm
meter

Fig.52. Plan of Wine Cellar with Jars

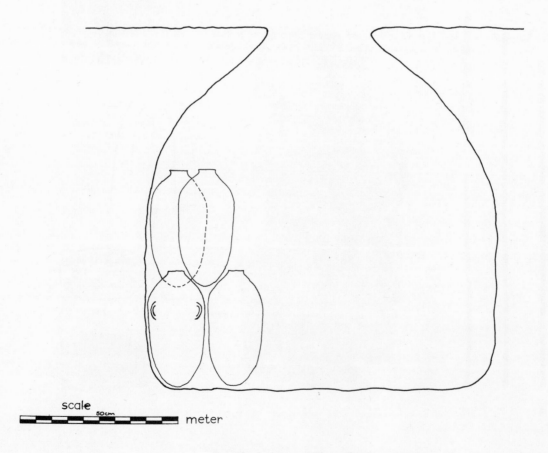

scale
50 cm
meter

Fig.53. Section of Wine Cellar with Jars

Fig.54. Openings to Cellars and Rock Cuttings in Area 8 Looking E.

Fig.55. Openings to Cellars and Rock Cuttings in Area 8 Looking SW.

Fig.56. Openings to Cellars and Rock Cuttings in Area 8 Looking E.

Fig.58. Opening of Loc. 105

and Rock Cutting 105a

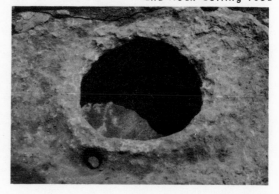

Fig.57. Opening to Loc. 105 and

Adjacent Rock Cutting in Area 8

Fig.59. Top of Limestone Block, No. 131

Fig. 60. Curbing of Loc. 104 Looking N.

Fig. 61. Openings to Cellars; Wall in 17-N-9 Looking W.

Fig.62. Opening to Cellars;
Walls in 17-P-10 Looking SW.

Fig.63. Openings to Cellars in
17-N-12 Looking SE.

Fig.64. Openings to Cellars and
Rock Cuttings in 17-M-10 Looking SE.

Fig.65. Opening to Loc. 216 and
Adjacent Rock Cutting Looking SE.

Fig.66. Rock Cuttings in 17-M-10,
Point 22, Looking SE.

Fig.67. Opening to Loc. 211 and Walls of Loc. 206 Looking SE.

Fig.68. Interior of Loc. 208, Wall and

Connecting Opening to Loc. 211, Looking N.

Fig.69. Opening and Cover of

Loc. 200 Looking E.

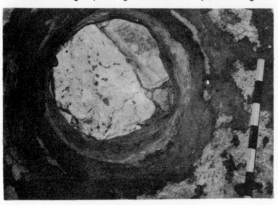

Fig.70. Ceiling and Cover of Cellar

in Loc. 138, Columbarium

Fig.71. Cover to Cellar in 18-G-4

Fig.72. Stairway to Loc. 138 Looking N.

Fig.73. Opening to Wine Cellars Cemented over Looking S.

Fig.74. East Wall of Tomb in Loc. 138, Showing Two Unfinished Arcosolia and Portion of Frieze

Fig.75. South Wall of Tomb in Loc. 138

Fig.76. Interior of Tomb in Loc. 138 Looking N.

Fig.77. Detail of Frieze from East Wall
of Tomb in Loc. 138

Fig.78. Frieze from Northern Part of
East Wall of Tomb in Loc. 138

Fig.79. Stone Door Found inside
of Tomb in Loc. 138

Fig.80. Neck of Northern Cellar in Columbarium in Loc. 138

Fig.81. Niches of the Columbarium in Loc. 138

Fig.82. Two Ovens in 10-M-3

Fig.83. Ramp in 10-M-4 Looking W.

Fig.84. Room with Pillars in 10-M-4 Looking W.

Fig.85. Ramp in 10-O-6 Looking E.

Fig.86. East Balk of 10-N-5

Showing Line of Ramp

Fig.87. Face of Foundation of Inner City Wall in 10-O-6 Looking NW.

Fig.88. City Wall in 17-R-13 Looking S.

Fig.89. Plaster Floor against Outer City Wall in 10-L-5 Looking NW.

Fig.90. Inner City Wall in 10-Q/R-8/9 Looking NE.

Fig.91. Storage Jars on Floor of Level 4a in 15-K-18 Looking W.

Fig.92. Three Partly Quarried Stones to the North of the Tell

Fig.93. House Area 17 Looking S.

Fig.94. Storage Bin at East
of Loc. 122 of House in Area 17

Fig.95. Court 123 in House
of Area 17 Looking N.

Fig.96. Rooms and Court of House in Area 17 Looking E.

Fig.97. Outer Face of City Wall in Trench I Looking W.

Fig.98. Roman Jar *in situ*
in Loc. 5 of Trench I

Fig.99. Roman Bath in Trench I Looking W.

Fig.100. City Wall in Trench I Looking NE.